# GARUDA & WINGED HORSES

## A JOURNEY THROUGH SIKKIM

# GARUDA & WINGED HORSES

## A JOURNEY THROUGH SIKKIM

Somnath Guha

Srishti Publishers & Distributors
64-A, Adhchini
Sri Aurobindo Marg
New Delhi 110017
First published by Srishti Publishers & Distributors in 2001


Rs.145.00
ISBN 81-87075-22-8

Cover Photography by Suvendu Chatterjee
Cover Design by Arrt Creations
45 Nehru Apartment, Kalkaji, New Delhi 110 019
e-mail: arrt@vsnl.com

Printed and bound in India by
Saurabh Print-O-Pack, Noida

**To My Father**

## Contents

# Acknowledgements

To Suva for going through my manuscript time and again.

To Babua for giving me access to his computer.

To my many Sikkimese friends who went out of their way to help and make this book possible.

# Ripples in the Sand

"When I was born, Sikkim was an independent country", said a young man to me at Rangpo, the 'gateway to Sikkim'. We were talking at the *haat*. It was market day at the border-town and people came from Melli, Kalijhora, Teestabazar and elsewhere to sell their wares - vegetables, groceries, sweets, cheap clothes, pakoras etc. Decibels were high and the river gurgled at a distance. To our right was a wooden house past its prime and yet vintage. On the first floor hung a variety of orchids. A lady, emaciated, almost invisible, sat in an armchair, her pale melancholy face glowing in the setting sun.

"You were seeing the orchids", the young man asked.

I didn't reply. I was still immersed in what he had just said : "when I was born, Sikkim was an independent country". How old would he be? Hardly 28-29. And yet deep within him there is anguish, an emptiness of a kingdom lost, a subtle resentment of an identity mutilated and hopelessly submerged. It is a feeling that he stubbornly refuses to admit, that it is there at all even if wrapped in the remotest corner of his consciousness. Like when I asked him about his nationality he replied that he is a Nepali but that first of all he is an Indian. Well adapted in the art of denying one's own feelings he had allowed himself just that one moment of indiscretion - just that one - and the snail had again withdrawn into its shell.

His father was a collector of orchids and watches. He was a contractor by profession. He even stood in an election and like the man he was, his symbol was rose. Outsiders who stop over at Rangpo enquire about his orchids.

"I have little knowledge about orchids nor do I have much interest", I admitted.

"Maybe he wants to photograph her", I said pointing to Suvendu.

Karki, the young man, took us into his house. There was no electricity. Creaky stairs, dark rooms, watches gleaming out of glass-framed cupboards, handicrafts peeping out of antique almirahs. As the shutter clicked, I drank squash.

It began to rain again. Vendors scurried for cover. Some pulled polythene sheets over their heads. The crowd thinned, the bazaar quietened, a stray dog whined unable to find room anywhere and repeatedly shook off rainwater from its body. Rain had accompanied us from the SNT bus stand at Siliguri. SNT is the acronym for "Sikkim Nationalized Transport" which came into existence in 1944 and which today is the largest source of revenue for the state. From here there are frequent bus services to Gangtok and other less frequent ones to Pelling and other places in the state. Rubbing shoulder with it is a trekkers' stand from which perilously packed vehicles, stumble out every now and then and nonchalantly head for scenic locations across the hills. Our destination was Ravang, which hardly anyone was interested in. If you were to go to Sikkim, Lachen, Pelling, Dzongri are the places to be in. Why waste time in a place where the sun is barely ever seen ? There is a one o'clock service we were told. And in the same breath cautioned that it is often cancelled owing to the lack of passengers. There are also maruti vans. "800 Rupees, off season price saab", chipped a twenty year old. Provocatively irreverent : jeans, cap, sneakers, key-ring-twirling-in-the-finger. We were on a shoe-string budget and could hardly afford to fritter our limited resources on such luxuries. Feeling the desolation of our pockets we recoiled under the shade pulling our luggage alongside. It was almost pouring by then. The day had turned murky and even the main road just ahead seemed to be in the distant horizon. Pelted by rain the trekkers' stand had turned into a mess. A few tourists who were hanging around had disappeared. The drivers and their staff were cocooned in their vehicles. Some slept, while some struck up a lazy conversation. A solitary trekker stood in the middle of the rectangle, half-full, its passengers bored with waiting. An equally bored driver sat at the wheel occasionally revving up the engine while a helper-boy had struck his head out crying "Gangtok, Gangtok". It was only ten o'clock then and the Ravang service three hours later seemed ages away. We had a terrible train journey, both of us sharing a berth and hardly having been able to sleep. What do we do? Wait and be damned? Or leave for Gangtok?

"Avail it. Get down at Singtam from where there is a regular service to Ravang", said the man at the counter as if he was reading our thoughts. "But you will have to pay the Gangtok fare". We found this to be an extra twenty rupees only and thus readily agreed. Even as we bought our tickets, small boys appeared from nowhere and deposited our luggage at the top of the trekker. We scurried behind and were told to occupy front seats. Suvendu sat by the window making room for his unwieldy legs. I rubbed water off my head, lit a cigarette and felt satisfied that somehow we had conjured up plump seats, which in Calcutta office-goers' parlance are "balcony ones". There were six others already seated out of which was a Bengali couple who by the look of their age were probably on a honeymoon trip. The young lady was worried. She was convinced that despite the polythene covers over her luggage, water was seeping into her bags. She prodded her husband to do something about it. She complained to the driver and occasionally turned towards us hoping we would help her. This went on for quite some time till her complaints got hysterical and a Hindustani trader was jolted into action. A couple of boys went up, did the necessary and assured the lady in mocking Bengali that everything was all right. Though she wasn't entirely convinced, her nagging stopped and silence fell in the courtyard apart for the constant pattering of rain.

Gradually the trekker filled up. Suvendu having mortgaged the window - side our monopoly of the front seat was attacked from the right. A man snuggled in beside me from the driver's side positioning his legs on either side of the gear. Soon the driver got in and the helper squeezed in on his right. By the time our vehicle lurched forward to clear a bump and take off for the highway, it was crammed with sixteen people with two at the back literally perched on the others. The euphoria over balcony seats was soon over. I felt my legs join, my body shrivel as if I was put to the grind in a compressor. Thankfully, inspite of the load our trekker raced past army camps on the outskirts of Siliguri, a railway crossing and began its climb towards the hills. The rain had lessened but it was still drip-dropping steadily. Arrows of light pierced through the horizon and sunbathed the road ahead. This is the national highway. Immediately ahead is Sevoke, the 'gateway of the wind' from where it branches off towards Guwahati, itself rising serpentinely towards Gangtok.

'Careful on my curves' read a 'Border Roads Organisation' graffiti along the highway. Someone in the BRO obviously has a cute sense of erotica. Of course he also has an idea of the vagaries of travel in this hilly state. From the foothills itself the river Teesta meanders alongside the road and the symphony flows past Gangtok, past Mangan, Lachen and Lachung in north Sikkim to Cholamoo from where it originates and from where Tibet is a whispering distance away. It runs the entire length of the state and the story of Teesta is the story of Sikkim. It twists and turns, rises and falls, hurtles over rocks, negotiates curves. At Berrick it is deep into the ravines, a silver lining, and yet menacing as it rumbles against the hills. At Kalijhora it is quietly flowing by, purring over obstacles, soft and sublime. At Goangaon in the north it metamorphoses into a glacier, a deadly and stealthily moving expanse of ice.

It's amazing to see the multifarious activities that

take place on a river-bed. Dhobis thrashed and washed clothes on stone slabs, rinsed them and hung them on ropes tied to bamboo poles dug into the sand. Trucks stood parked by narrow streams as the driver and the *khalasis* enjoyed a much needed wash. A little distance away women labourers quarried stones while some others dumped them into the truck's behind. At one point a billboard announced river-rafting at another a placard announced eco-picnic-spots. Come winter the entire stretch of the river-bed from Sevoke to Kalijhora is under siege. Revellers from the plains, from the towns of Siliguri, Jalpaiguri, Coochbehar, gather in hordes, in buses, trucks and tempos and transform the area into a veritable joyland. The highway is then thick with vehicles. The Sevoke temple crowded with devotees. The monkeys along the road have more to eat then, what with the picnickers disposing of loaves of bread and bananas, their staple breakfast, to the waiting langoors. Shamianas are put up all over the river bank. Durrees are spread on sand on which ladies seat, gossip and play housey. Their menfolk play rummy and the more adventurous fish in the Teesta. Soon the air is filled up with delicious aromas ——— *bhetki* being fried, chicken roasted, benign brinjals turned into crisp, munchy *begunis.* The air is also heavy with the smell of liquor and as microphnes blared out the latest popular numbers, the young and the old swing to the rhythm and the carnival reaches its crescendo.

We crossed Kalijhora, Teestabazar, Melli. The rain had stopped and a jaded sun blinked on the horizon trying valiantly to light up the hills. The surroundings were still struggling to come to terms with daily life. Wisps of smoke rose from huts perched on the slopes. Men and women were repairing roads. Some with baskets of logs on their backs walked laboriously to their destinations. The road was slippery and was made more dangerous by the numerous falls that were overflowing. The couple chattered but most of the others had fallen into a slumber. Enamoured with the surroundings we remained slumped in our seats.

# Sighs and Soul-Searching

We were jolted out of our seats at Rangpo. The driver got out ; he announced a break of fifteen minutes. Everyone headed for the café selling tea, coffee, cakes and biscuits. We were tired. We had had a terrible night in the train with both of us sleeping in the same bunk and neither getting a good sleep . We got out and stretched ourselves and looking back over our shoulders we saw the beautiful Tibetan-architectured bungalow. It was past noon then and the sun still glistened over the canopy. I watched the luggage and Suvendu rushed to enquire if there was any accommodation available. The entire bungalow was empty and we checked into it. We had a nap and then wandered into the market and Karki's house when it began to pour again leaving us stranded for quite a long time. The lady who was being photographed looked unhappy. Her husband who stood at the door looked sick. An engineer who had graduated from Okhla, he stays well when he is in north Sikkim where he is posted. Down at Rangpo the heat gets to him. Karki himself looked depressed. Like his father he is a man of many interests. He is a timber-trader and an avid angler —— the only one in the town, he boasts. His catch is mostly *mahasher* ,a kind of *rui* and *asala*, a kind of trout. He is also a collector of hats, a handicraft -maker and has a welding certificate.

"Why welding ?" I asked.

"Because I can make aircrafts and fly them. I have no friends —— I want to go foreign". Rain, darkness and a woman fragile and forlorn. Flickering shadows of lamp, the sound of *zunkeri*, crickets —— like the tinkering of coke bottles in a railway compartment.

"Why don't you seek employment here ?"

"I tried to start a business at Siliguri. But people are very conservative. They intrude into your private lives".

Such is the way of life. Tired and worn out, you seek out a corner of heaven. You find it at Rangpo —— god-gifted, nature-bathed, river-washed. There you find a young man, burdened with ambition, wanting to leave, moving away from his beautiful place, across frontiers to another land to pursue a trade as practical and dreary as welding.

That night Karki saw us off at the bungalow. It was past eight, which was quite late by Sikkim standards. Raju served our dinner in the room which we had luckily ordered before we left in the afternoon. Later we sat at the balcony which hangs almost precariously over the river. To the right is the arch that ushers one into the state. To the left are three petrol pumps and numerous liquor shops and bars and eateries. Just in front and almost under your nose is the river. It is the Rangpo river, Rangpokhola as the locals call it - *khola* meaning canal. It is a river lean and thin for most of the year. The river bed is largely barren : a sweeping strech of chips, stones and boulders. Naughty and enthusiastic streams break away from the main course, form ponds and puddles and exhaust themselves in the unyielding expanse of sand. In them children play and bathe, women wash utensils, scrub clothes, dip their hair, and nonchalantly undress and slip into dry clothes. Down below on the western side the Rangpokhola meets the Teesta. It is a haven for fishing and bird-watching and one could drown in the silence of nature.

Next morning Karki came early and we went to the confluence of the rivers, walking through people's houses, alleys, playing-fields, sand-beds, rocks. To our left on the other side of the river is the Darjeeling district of West Bengal where the Gorkhaland agitation erupted in the nineteen eighties. Border areas like Rangpo were then good shelters for agitators wanting to avoid the police.

"I made some quick money then", Karki said with

a hint of smile. "They sold logs at dirt-cheap prices", the smile broadened.

It had rained through out the night. The surroundings were wet, the hills lush green. The sun hidden behind a veil of cloud. Karki looked more fresh than yesterday but there was no missing that shadow of depression.

"So you are doing pretty well here, at least financially", Suvendu asked in between taking snaps and grumbling about the weather not being conducive to good photography.

"Yes, money has never been a problem. But there is lack of good company". There was frustration of being cocooned in a small place, of not being able to give expression to one's talents.

"People are very corrupt. All Indians are corrupt; didn't the British say it a long time ago ?".

So bloody what ! I felt like saying. Seven o'clock in the morning at Rangpo is hardly the setting to discuss corruption.

"Sikkim is the most corrupt state. All government people are corrupt. Even my brother is corrupt".

The venom in his voice startled me. Unfortunately all the ills of the Indian society, down to shitting on river beds, have been duplicated and magnified manifold in this small state. Everytime I went back I heard new scandals regarding lottery, housing, school text-books and uniforms. The politicians make pots of money while the population at large remain steeped in poverty. Raju, the barman or Paula, the durwan earn a measly Rs. 700 a month working for unlimited hours at the guest house.

"You are an angry young man", I told him while we were walking back.

"Actually I have no friends here. I want to go into tourism. Rafting and fishing can be encouraged here. Why don't you promote me ?" he beseeched.

This is a common problem I have faced during my years of freelancing. People think you are big. That you have the right contacts and can get things done.

"We could bring out a piece on Rangpo. We could insert your name as the person to contact here. I am afraid that's the best we could do."

He smiled sadly. I thought there was pity in his eyes, almost ridicule, the dawning of the realization that he had spent time on us barely for nothing. Nevertheless he shook hands, took our visiting cards and walked down the *haat* road. He was in a hurry. He had to take his mother to Siliguri for a medical check-up.

Later in the day we loitered aimlessly at the chowk area. It had 13 wine shops and at least 3 of them were stacked with the best and the costliest brands in the business. Even Esplanade in Calcutta does not have the stock that they have here. Who are the buyers ? The tourists ? "Tourists yes. Local people also buy", said a trader sitting at the counter. An acquaintance who came here way back in 1966 told us that there was only one shop then selling Black Cat, the ubiquitous Sikkimese rum. It smells of the wooden vats in which it is prepared and though its taste was repelling to me, it is said to be the most coveted drink for the connoisseurs of rum. It is the earliest instance of Sikkimese entrepreneurship and is in that sense the symbol of Bhutia royalty and the Buddhist milieu that had been the essence of the state. It is at this chowk area that the demise of that royalty and the rise of a new political class, Nepali-dominated and backed by India, began. Twenty-five years ago it was here that Sikkim's history took a violent turn and landed the tiny kingdom into the lap of its giant neighbour. The anti-monarchy agitation of 1973 led to the signing of the path-breaking May 8 agreement. Among other things it provided for a legislative assembly elected on the basis of adult franchise and safeguards for minorities which would specifically ensure that no single group amongst the Bhutias, Lepchas and Nepalis would assume a dominant position in the society. Under this provision the new assembly consisted of 32 members out of which 15 were reserved for the Bhutia-Lepchas and one for the monks, who at that time numbered nearly 2000 spread in far-flung and remote monasteries in the state. Out of the remaining seats, 15 were reserved for the Sikkimese Nepalis and one for scheduled castes. This is the traditional 'Parity System' followed since the British period. With the signing of this new agreement Palden Namgyal, the Chogyal or the Maharaja of Sikkim became a figurehead, a constitutional dummy atop a house of elected members. For all practical purposes power vested with the Chief Executive appointed by Delhi. In matters of dispute between the Chogyal and the C.E. the latter's or rather Delhi's was the last word. Only the palace establishment and the Sikkim Guards were directly under the monarch's control. Thus a dynasty which took roots way back in 1642, which lived through numerous Nepali and Bhutanese aggressions and British subjugation, the vicissitudes which forced the rulers to shift capital numerous times, was finally in its last throes. The clamour for democracy had rose when British left India in 1947. As princely states all over the country merged with the mother nation, the Sikkim congress led by the indefatigable Kazi Lhendup Dorzi who continued to lead the party for another 30 years, raised the banner of revolt. Their demand : democracy and even merger with India. India then sided with Tashi Namgyal, the then Chogyal, father of Palden. Its forces actually helped put down the revolt. That was in 1950 and India was still flushed with the hope and excitement of independence. It understood the agony of being a colony and it cherished the sweetness of freedom. Moreover international relations too were favourable then. 'Hindi-Chini Bhai-Bhai' was on everyone's lips and China had not yet cast its evil designs on Tibet. The Himalayan region was peaceful. Nepal, Bhutan and Sikkim served as a conglomerate of buffer states, forming a comfortable cushion between India and China. India then was the leader of non-aligned nations and spoke up for other's freedom. In keeping with its stature it signed a treaty with Sikkim granting it protectorate status. The arrangements worked well for nearly 20 years till anti-monarchy agitation began to gain momentum and culminated in the May 8 agreement.

Elections to the new assembly were held in April, 1974 and the Sikkim Congress swept to power winning 31 out of the 32 seats. The National Party backed by the Chogyal won only one seat. What came as a surprise to observers then was that it failed to win any of the BL seats (the 15 seats reserved for the Bhutia-Lepchas, communities which staunchly backed the Namgyal regime) and what's more even the Sangha Seat in spite of the fact that Chogyal was not only the temporal head but also the religious head of Sikkim. This was partly because many monasteries were in bad shape, grants had dried up and monks were largely dissatisfied with the regime. However the National Party's debacle in the BL seats was expected. The demographic situation even then in the state was such that the Nepalis were an overwhelming majority in the East, West and South Districts. Only in the North were the BLs more numerous thanks to the restrictions on other communities to settle there. But then the North had and even today has only 3 constituencies. In other reserved constituencies the Nepalis by virtue of being more in number decided the fate of a candidate and as an influential political leader in post-merger Sikkim said : "the merger happened because the Nepalis wanted it". Simply put, Nepalis no longer enjoyed being ruled by a king from another community. Thus the BLs were helpless even in their own constituencies as the Nepali vote was and till today is the decisive factor. This also effectively meant the death of the May 8 agreement at its very inception. All those talk of safeguards for minorities, of ethnic balance, of not allowing any particular community to acquire a dominant position went for a six as the Nepalis by virtue of their brute majority called the shots not only in politics but also in other spheres of life. In that sense though the merger occurred in 1975, the process of that merger began decades ago when the first intrepid Nepali peasants entered the land, fanned out into the countryside, into uninhabited areas, began terrace-cultivation and through their sheer hard work and industriousness became a vital clog in Sikkim's development. Migrants always do better than locals simply because they start from zero. In West Bengal people who came from the then East Pakistan (now Bangladesh) began as refugees living in makeshift, congested colonies. Later they went places, and outpaced the West Bengalis in various fields. Unlike the later, the *Bangal*s, as these people came to be known, didn't have the luxury of going back to their ancestral land and property simply because those were now in another country's territory. They started from zero and their survival instincts were that much stronger. The Chogyals and later the British and the Indian Government welcomed the Nepalis because they were willing to take up odd jobs and get into agriculture which the locals were reluctant to do. Perhaps this was no calculated population exchange or displacement as we have heard is being done in Tibet. Whatever, in time to come it boomeranged, as the Nepalis far outgrew the indigenous population which finally spelt the doom of the dynasty and paved the way for the merger.

The sky opened up again. A persistent drizzle, a constant drip-drip, a mist over the river, the police chowki a silhouette and a day in perennial coma. There were hardly any other people at the guest house and that is the way it is for most of the year. Rooms are reasonable here. Rs. 330 for a double bed and Rs. 550 for AC. Unimaginable at Gangtok considering the originality and splendor of the bungalow's design. Raju works as a barman and also doubles up as an attendant. His father works at a local distillery and earns Rs. 1200 a month. His brothers cultivate the bit of land that the family has. Raju's home is near by but Paulas' some distance away. Up and down he walks for nearly 14 kms. everyday, to attend to his eight -to-eight job, to earn a paltry Rs. 700. Hard grind really. But was it better during the Chogyal's time?

"*Raja ke samay acchcha tha*", the old man grinned. It was a poor man's frank admission.

"What did you do then?"

"Carried goods from here to Singtam and further upwards".

"How ?".

"On my back", he said turning around and still smiling. And he went on to add that any nuisance was tackled by whip—wielding *kazi's* men who patrolled the road.

Barbaric! almost Uncle Tom's Cabin and this man has the cheek to say that Raja's time was better. There is no serfdom now, no bonded labour as was then practiced by the ruthless kazis. At least men like Paula have a job, a job with honour, however low-yielding it is.

"*Phir bhi acchcha tha*", Paula continued to smile and repeat.

He couldn't care less about what all I said. No logic, no arguments, no philosophical humbug about people's participation in power, about democracy's superiority over monarchy, about adult franchise and individual freedom, about the necessity of land reforms as against sprawling private estates would convince the likes of Paula that they are living under a better system of governance today. That is faith for you, the sheer simplicity of which shields it from the onslaught of reason or knowledge or even progress, makes it as rock-solid and unwavering as Kanchenjungha, the mountain deity, the Holy Grail which all of Sikkim worship. There have been several other occasions when I have heard that line being said : *Raja ke samay acchcha tha*". An impoverished Nepali coolie begging me for a peg of rum at the Ganesh Tok jocularly repeated the line every-time I pointed out to him the many developments that have taken place since 1975. Well-to-do Bhutias aired the same feelings, as did numerous young men in Gangtok and elsewhere. An elderly gentleman one Mr. Dorji, scion of one of the oldest and much respected families in the north told me at his house at Mangan : "Unfortunately

India didn't handle Chogyal very well". We had just returned from a tiresome journey and rested in his vast drawing room. We sat on low sofas and in front of us were small tables called *chokseys* on which was served *chhang*, in bamboo pipes called *kodo*, a heady millet brew which is offered when guests come calling. On another choksey was kept a tumbler of hot water which is occasionally mixed with the brew to keep it working. Tradition has it that one has to at least have a sip of chhang as a mark of respect to the host. We did and as I looked around, surprise ! surprise ! I found an impressive photograph of Mrs. Indira Gandhi hung on the wall. Mrs. Gandhi's photograph in a traditional Bhutia-Buddhist family's house, a family which was close to Chogyal, a relationship for which Dorji had to live in exile for months after the merger. Mrs. Gandhi whom all of Sikkim blame for the events of 1973-75. Mrs. Gandhi whose arrogance, headstrongness, paranoia bulldozed Sikkim's protectorate status to dust, dumped its royal family to permanent isolation. Paradoxically again, Dorzi blasted the local political parties, the Sikkim Sangram Parishad (SSP) and the 'Sikkim Democratic Front' (SDF) . "Congress is our only hope. Only Congress can give security to my community, bring development in Sikkim". As if Congress and Chogyal are the same side of the same coin. But again when it came to matters of the royal family, his voice dropped. "India *ne* Chogyal *ke saath acchcha nahin kiya*", tears welled up in his eyes.

"Prince Wangchuk is living in poverty. He has no servants. He has to even cook his own food".

Wangchuk is Palden Namgyal's second son born of his first marriage. The elder son died in a car crash. Palden Namgyal himself died of cancer in 1982.

I didn't believe him. Of course after power and kingdom were taken away their earnings dropped. But even now there are areas marked with billboards reading '*property of Chogyal Wangchuk Namgyal'*. Even now the family has enough estates, enough in its coffers. Everyone knows it; it's common knowledge. Moreover a compensation claim made by the late Chogyal is due to be settled soon. In 1979 the claim was pegged at Rs. 110 crores. However fresh assessments are being made by a high-level Indian delegation and the family's lawyers and the claim could be paid shortly. Dorji sensed that I wasn't convinced.

"Chogyal had nothing", he whispered in all earnestness. "It is we people who sustained him. Like when he came to Mangan I presented him gifts — say a piece of my estate — as a mark of respect".

There is love, veneration, a groundswell of sympathy for the Chogyal everywhere. It could be interpreted in many ways. Most want a space to be found for the Chogyal's successors in the present political set up. *JO WADA KIYA HAI NIVANA PAREGA* —— promises that have been made must be kept. They want strict implementation of the May 8 agreement, which they feel, will ensure Sikkim's special place within the Indian union.

# Rain and Ravangla

Next day somehow we shook off the magnetic hold that Rangpo was having on us and headed for Ravang. The weather remained treacherous. There were landslides on the road to Gangtok. Vehicles were taking a detour to reach the capital. The road to Ravang, however, was safe. Our trip to that place, known as the 'Cherrapunji of Sikkim', originated from a chance meeting with D.D. Bhutia, a senior minister of the SDF government at the Sikkim house in Calcutta. Uttam Lepcha whom I had befriended when I had been to Gangtok to cover the 1994 elections was in Calcutta. One morning during that election he had walked up to me at the lobby of hotel Tibet. He was flashy, handsome and seemed to be in a hurry for glory.

"Why don't you stay at my hotel ? We can have a nice time together."

I was on an assignment with a television channel which now specialises in religious sermons. Our crew was leaving for Calcutta that day and I was staying back for the results. I had the option to choose my hotel. I chose his simply because it would help me to get acquainted with a Sikkimese person and also because I liked him. It helped me forge a relationship that exists till today. Uttam had contested the election but lost badly. It took him months to recover from the drubbing. Then he started a studio for which he has the right credentials as he is a fine photographer. He had gone to Bombay and on his return home was staying for a couple of days at the Sikkim house in Calcutta. He had called us over for dinner. We spent the evening sheaving through his portfolio, and admiring beautiful nature photographs shot mainly in west and south Sikkim.

We met D.D. Bhutia in the lobby. We talked politics and the controversial hydro-electric project that was coming up at Yoksum. It was much in news then. It was the first false move made by the SDF government since it came to power. The 30MW hydel project at Rathong Chu created a furore in the state. Yoksum is the place from where one begins the fabulous treks to Dzongri and Gochala. Once upon a time it was also the capital of the Namgyal dynasty. It is considered to be a *LHAKHANG*, house of gods, where Sikkim's deities dwell. There are said to be many sacred locations and hidden treasures in the area, the significance of which is only understood by senior enlightened lamas. There are several monasteries in the area. A few kms away is the

Pemayangtse monastery of the Nyingma sect which is one of the most stately gompas in the state. Close by is Rabdantse, entirely in ruins, and which too had been the seat of the dynasty. It is a zone of rich biodiversity wrapped in intriguing history, myths and legends. The project would wipe off rare flora and fauna, endanger wildlife, inundate vast areas of thick forest coverage and destroy invaluable Buddhist relics. Most of all it would breach the centuries old tranquility that looms over the place, the splendid isolation in which monasteries thrive, the mist-heavy quiet in which whispering monks float through their daily chores.

All of Sikkim was concerned about the project. The lamas in particular were on the warpath. Politicians of all hues joined issue. Danny Denzappa a well known actor of Bollywood, a son of the soil, voiced his disapproval. Environmentalists from all over the country made a beeline for Yuksom. The issue landed the government in a tight spot.

Obviously the minister was in much discomfort whenever we brought up the subject. He is a tall and sturdy man and like all hill people simple and very likable. Sikkim needs development, it needs industrialization, he argued. These people are holding up development, he said.

Later the discussion veered to other subjects and

he asked us to visit Ravang which is his native place and also adjacent to his constituency Ralong. "Come during Panglhabsol, our national festival. You will enjoy it", he had said. It was he who led us to Kishore Ghosh and hotel Mainam.

"Ghosh and madam convinced us that it would be a good tourist spot". Madam is Kishoreda's wife who is a teacher of English at the local school. "We asked them to start a hotel. We provided them all help"' Bhutia had said admiringly.

We were received well at the hotel. A TV sent out erratic pictures, 3-days old newspaper lay on a table, a board with pasted pictures announced the sight - seeing spots around Ravang. As we gorged ourselves with plates full of toast and omelettes Kishoreda related to us how he was trying to make this an attractive tourist spot. It mainly started with the SDF Government coming to power in 1994. Having won substantial number of seats in south district, the new government was out to develop these areas. A branch of the SBI (State Bank of India) was already in place. STD booth was installed at a stationery shop though often it is impossible to get through to Gangtok or Siliguri, leave alone distant Calcutta. The one o'clock trekker service from Siliguri also came into being. The hotel itself began to function in 1995. In Sikkim no outsider is allowed to possess any property. The Ghosh family took the hotel on lease and has been running it ever since. On their own they organized features in various publications. It needed quite some doing on their part for Ravang with a small population and tucked away in a remote corner was hardly on the tourist map of Sikkim. Later in bureaucratic circles of Gangtok we heard people exclaiming, "You have been to Ravang!" Gradually their efforts began to pay dividends. People in Calcutta came to know about the place and tourists began to trickle in.

After we had our fill, we decided to look at the place by ourselves. Outside it drizzled softly and it was very cold. Standing at the entrance to the hotel Kishoreda gave us a sketch of the surroundings. On our right was the power complex, its lights like Diwali bulbs hanging precariously against the backdrop of silhouetted hills. On our left towards the trekkers' stand was a row of shops, bars and restaurants, wine shops and groceries. Ahead down a slope or two was the market above which rose the imposing Mainam hill.

"A weekly haat is held on Wednesdays", Kishoreda told us.

I had a view of it during my next visit. I found old women, their ears and noses burdened with oversized, cumbersome rings, their faces the most inscrutable, intricate of maps. They come from as far as 10-12 kms.

away, walking, to sell their meagre produce like potato, ginger or cardamom.

"We have advised the government to make it more attractive by selling handicrafts, paintings and woodwork by local artists", Kishoreda informed enthusiastically. Perhaps finding that we were not warming up to the economics of the area, he switched on to something more sublime.

"In the morning if you stand here and look east the entire range will stare on your face. It is a breathtaking vision of mount Kanchenjungha and the associate peaks Karbu, Pandim and Tahun".

Kishoreda asked us to take an escort but we moved on. Immediately ahead on the left hand side we entered a bar. An attractive lady manned the counter which was stocked with a whole range of liquor bottles. The entire inner space was cabinned, heavily draped. We asked for whiskey and toyed with the peg. The man who served us was extremely courteous. Short and diffident looking, he appeared within minutes with a plate of steaming momos.

"Have it. It goes well with the drink", he whispered.

"Why don't you join us?" I asked. He started and looked at the counter. The lady was gone. The street looked deserted. It was about seven and Ravang had begun its preparations for the night.

His name was Dawa Bhutia. He poured us another whiskey and hovered around our table.

“You seem to be educated !”

He looked a bit puzzled quite unsure of himself.

“Yes way back in 1952 in the Scottish Missionary School of Kalimpong”.

“You belong to this place?”

“Yes, from Lingtam in Borong which is a few kms. from here”.

“How was Ravang then?”

Dawa thought for some time.

“It was all jhopri then. I am talking of 1970. Tibetan refugees cleared the jungle and settled here and then came the Nepalese”.

Our liquor was disappearing fast. Momos had become cold and tasteless. Suvendu went out into the street looking for photo-opportunities.

“What was the situation here like during the anti-Chogyal agitation ?”

“I wasn’t here then”.

“On which side were you. Pro or anti-merger?”

“Don’t know. Never been interested in politics”. Then looking straight into my eyes said : “It’s better that you don’t bring up such subjects.”

Suddenly his mildness evaporated and with a firm

gait he disappeared into the kitchen.

It was quite some time before he appeared again. With more drinks and more momos. I was appalled.

"Who is going to have all this", I said, rather subdued.

"Have it", Dawa chided me. "Liquor is cheap here. I will make it cheaper for you'.

Having got a rebuff I searched for ways to pick up the conversation. Dawa sat on Suvendu's chair and as I sipped I felt his eyes roving all over me.

"First time at Ravang?"

I nodded my head.

"Tourist, or for some other purpose ?

"Writing."

"Writing what ?"

"Don't know. Not sure as yet ." I looked up at him. The interviewer had become interviewee but I sensed that he was back to his old genial self. He leapt up from his chair as Suvendu entered.

"What are the places to be seen here ?" he asked.

Dawa reeled off a list of names. Suvendu scrubbed his hair and took a long sip.

"But what use if the weather remains like this".

It can really be frustrating for a photographer in such situations. Rain and mist can muck up your best shots. It can spoil your entire trip.

We drank late into the evening. We went back only when Kishoreda sent one of his boys to fetch us. Dawa taught at a school near Rumtek in east Sikkim. He came back in 1984 and took to cultivation in his ancestral farm. He is also a share-holder of the restaurant.

As we were leaving Dawa suddenly grabbed my arm : "Smash and Grab", he whispered, his voice almost inaudible. I was surprised.

After that rebuff we were talking places, culture, food. No politics. 'Smash and Grab - the Annexation of Sikkim' is the celebrated book written by Sunanda Dutta Ray. People in Sikkim talk admiringly about it. A few have reservations as well.

Luckily next morning the weather was clear. Kishoreda arranged a vehicle for us and we were off. Shankar our young driver talked non-stop. There was a man who stayed for months at the forest lodge studying birds and butterflies. Another who remained locked in his room, writing the entire day. "It is me who takes the tourists to sight-seeing trips, who guides them on the mountain trek", he boasted. Perhaps he was trying to figure out in which category we belonged.

The hills were sun-drenched, the peaks gleaming majestically. The huts on hill terraces clear and sharp. The road wet but getting drier by the minute. Blades of glass shone, their tips lustrous with overnight rain.

Such weather lifts everybody's spirits. So it did for Suvendu. Occasionally our vehicle would stop and he would stroll around for shots. Occasionally our vehicle would stop for other reasons as well. To pick up people and drop them. School-teachers, office goers, people going to relative's house and even labourers. In between attending to us, Shankar would talk to them. About how the school was doing, about the crop and the weather, about prices, about the post-office that was to be opened at Ravang. They would get down at their destinations and depart with a grin and a wave of hands. No money paid, none asked for. How adversity brings the best out of men ! In the interiors where people have to walk miles to go to their workplaces, to bring their provisions, it is Samaritans like Shankar who keep the wheel of life moving, make life that bit easier for the inhabitants.

We went to the Ralong monastery. It is one of the most historic shrines in Sikkim. It is in bad shape. A new one is coming up and it is being built on a grand scale. It is slated to become a Buddhist University. Construction Work was going on everywhere. Carpentry and masonry sounds echoed around the building. Lama officials were supervising the work. Lama children looked curiously at Suvendu taking photographs, performed their chores, played and occasionally vanished into the alleys in the hills. One son in every Buddhist family joins lamadom. That is how the age-old order is sustained.

Ralong monastery has a story behind it. It is said that lamas of Tibet ordered a gumpha to be built in Sikkim. Their message was to scour the jungle and peaks and to find out the spot where a goat will emerge from the bush and stand. At that exact spot the monastery was to come up. The name Ralong originates from the story. 'Ra' meaning goat and 'long' meaning to stand. The story goes on further. For the house-warming ceremony of the new monastery lamas of Tibet were supposed to come and do the puja. However due to circumstances beyond their control, they were refused permission to come. Instead the holy men sent birds carrying grains. These fell on the laps of lamas of Ralong thus sanctifying their puja. Some of the old lamas are still said to possess these grains.

That evening we met Chewang Dorji Bhutia. Lots of people knew his bio-data by heart. A contractor by profession, owner of five hills, educated in Darjeeling and a topper in political science from North Bengal University.

"A Gold medallist in Political Science", Dawa told us.

"He can tell you everything about the place",

Kishoreda informed.

"He is my landlord, the only educated man at Ravang", said Shyamal Dutta, the Branch Manager of SBI.

We met him at Duttada's flat. He was fiftyish, dignified and a man of few words. We knew he has a tragic past. One fateful evening driving to Siliguri in a maruti, his family had a fatal accident. He escaped unhurt but both his wife and son died on the spot. All night he kept a vigil over the dead frantically trying in between to draw the attention of passing vehicles. It was only in the wee hours of the morning that a military truck came to his help and carried the dead to Siliguri hospital. As expected the incident devastated him. It made him a complete wreck. "What pains him most is that the accident occurred in trying to overtake. He believes he killed his own family. He just cannot forgive himself", Duttada had told us. The man entirely keeps to himself and has never again taken to the wheels.

Having heard all this we felt a bit awed to open up in his presence. Time went by in exchanging pleasantries or just sitting quiet.

He saved us from the awkwardness by starting the conversation himself.

"I know why you have been wanting to talk to me. But I am afraid I can't tell you much. Why don't you read 'The Sikkim Gazetteer'. It has a lot of information".

I kept quiet wanting him to proceed.

"There are other books also. But that is the most authentic".

"You are very respected here".

"Oh, it's nothing much", he said, a hint of a smile on his face.

"You could have pursued a career elsewhere".

"Could have, yes. I did some teaching but then I had to come back and take charge of my family estate".

We had heard a familiar story from Dawa the previous evening. How often I was to hear that many more times in various parts of Sikkim. A young man creating waves in interior decoration in Delhi returns to take charge of his estate in remote Mangan. An engineer doing well in Mumbai returns for the same reason. Bright young men who can take on the best in any field return to the confines of their native land making a mockery of all their talent and capabilities. Why back to farming after all the education, back to reclaiming a feudal heritage after having snapped links with the system. "Does this tendency continue? This tendency to return to the roots even when one has the opportunity to make good elsewhere?" He thought for sometime, looked up and then shaking his head said, "Can't say for sure."

Time passed, Suvendu fiddled with an old newspaper. Duttada had switched on the TV at a low volume. A perky young lady was sailing through a news bulletin on a satellite channel.

"Hardly anyone went for education in my days"' the landlord took us back in time.

"Could be we could not adjust to the climate, the hot plains, also the atmosphere : it was very competitive out there."

He fell into brooding. The sound of drizzle and Duttada's tinkering with crockery in the kitchen. Shifting images on the TV, a commercial ——lama boy ecstatic over the quality of a cycle.

"You cannot imagine today how difficult it was to go to Siliguri in those days". There was almost melancholy in his voice.

"Going to the plains was quite an occasion in the family. Get a vehicle, arrange a place to stay, get the right clothes, get mentally prepared to interact with a different kind of people. They could always take you for a ride, you know"' he laughed.

The great psychological barrier, the wide gulf between the hills and the plains. Could development bridge this great divide, the fear and suspicion about the plains. For Ravang it would perhaps take another decade to address this question. By that time students at the local high school, who are first generation learners, would come of age. The town too would possibly develop into a bustling hill-station.

Social or emotional barriers did not prevent one man from defying the odds. Born and brought up at Ravang, he had never stepped out of the hills till he took the giant step of enrolling in the Gorkha brigade chasing glory and fortune elsewhere. The soldier never looked back thereafter. He performed with rare courage and distinction at the Burma front and was wounded in 1942. His greatest moment came in 1944 when he was awarded the Victoria Cross by the British Government. After independence he remained with the Indian army though he had the option to go over to Britain. At that time it was impossible for the local inhabitants for whom even Siliguri was light years away, to realize the drive of a man who had scoured the entire country and even ventured abroad. One who had gone places, jostled with the high and mighty, witnessed earth - shattering events. The soldier grew in years, served in various capacities won more laurels and on retirement returned to the quietness of the hills. Yet few of the locals recognized his worth. It was only recently that someone woke upto it and brought the man out of the closet. Gonju Lama is today Ravang's hottest property, it's only celebrity, an astonishing instance of how human will in one generation's time, can overcome centuries of isolation.

V.C. Saab as he is popularly known, does not meet people without prior appointment. We sent a message and went to his house in the evening. It was a blustery day with the usual raindrops spattering us on the face. True to his status the old man maintains a dignified distance from others. His house situated atop a hillock stands in splendid solitude to the rest of the town. Tall pine trees around his farm form a boundary shutting out the town. Only the glow of the lights in the town below formed a nimbus in the sky assuring one that civilization is not too for away.

There was a cowshed and some tin-roofed cottages for drying *elaichi*. On the slopes were several huts, the workers' busti. The old man stood in his gravelled courtyard with a minion holding aloft an umbrella. We were led into the sitting room and settled into sofas. He sat across us and with a wave of his hands sent others out of the room.

I looked around and found that we were in a museum of sorts. Almost the entire wall opposite us was covered with photographs. Below them were exquisite wooden tables and chokseys on which were displayed medals, trophies and plaques, all ostensibly won for some kind of valor or other. On the left was a big cupboard filled with pamphlets and books. There was a whole row of certificates interspersed with khukris and more medals and photos. There were many photographs as well including those of the Chogyal and President Radhakishnan, Zakir Hussain and V.V.Giri. Gonju Lama was sprawled on his seat, his arms spread over the top and a broad contented smile across his face. The lights were dim, so much so that eyes hurt. The wind was howling outside and the atmosphere was eerie.

"Voltage is always fluctuating here. *Kuch kam nahi karte hai yeh log*", V.C. Saab observed.

"But down below the lights are stable", I made a feeble attempt to bail out the electricity people.

"They reason that because of the height supply is poor. These government people are no good.

"Earlier people were better?" I asked sensing some resentment in what he had said.

"*Raja ka samay acchcha tha*", he said with a quiet finality.

Interestingly many in Sikkim refer to the Chogyal as Raja. I have found a clear divide in this. While the educated and the well-to-do prefer Chogyal (Gonju Lama being an exception), the common people in general use Raja. It is said that at the insistence of his American wife Hopecook, Palden Namgyal insisted on being called as Chogyal. Maharaja and Maharani were too subservient, too much smacking of India. Hopecook herself took up the title Gyalmo, the royal consort. This became another source of friction in the already uneasy relationship between India and Sikkim then.

"Hasn't there been a lot of development?"

"*Kya* development, only electricity has come. Rest all are same".

"But I thought you have come to talk about me", he said with irritation. We shifted uneasily in our seats and exchanged glances.

"What influenced you to join the army?"

"A cousin was already in the army. He was a big influence. Moreover in those days there was nothing to do here".

"He took you for recruitment".

"No. British Officials used to come to the villages looking for healthy young men. They selected me ".

"You were recruited on spot?"

"No Recruitment center was then at Ghoom. *Kuch nahin tha*. No transport. I went walking, whole day, via Jorethang".

Even today people of remote areas are scared of even going to Siliguri. That is hardly their fault. Even now school children are taken to the town because they have never seen a train in their lives. All the more commendable that this man had the drive and initiative to go on his own to that distant center in Darjeeling district.

"There a sahib was writing down names. My original name is Gyamtsho, he put it down as Gonju. And they used to think that all Buddhists are lamas and I became Gonju Lama"' the old man roared with laughter.

The British always had this, this uncanny ability to improvise oriental names to suit their own purpose.

There was a painting on the wall showing Gonju Lama involved in a tank fight. I drew his attention to it .

"Oh, that is the battle that earned me the V.C. Single-handedly I destroyed two tanks. Everybody says the Japanese are brave. But even they were not good enough for me".

"Tell us about the battle."

"*Bahut din ho gaya*. That was long time ago. We were under heavy machine gun fire. I went ahead of my force. Suddenly I got shot, in my thighs and left hand. My gun fell down. I saw the tanks approaching. I couldn't even bring out my grenades. Somehow I managed and threw them, four in all. They landed hardly a few meters away. The whole earth went up and I remained dumped. Enemy retreated, my force came to my rescue", he said in one breath.

"This was at which front?"

"Burma. *Le kar phek diya*. After 6 months' training".

"That got you the V.C?"

"Yes, Rifleman of 7, Gorkha Rifles, Gonju Lama leading the parade on a wheelchair. That was on 24-10-44. Lord Wavell himself was present."

Later he was associated with VC reunions and worked towards helping retired soldiers. He visited England several times, met the queen and had dinner at the Buckingham Palace.

"Those photographs of the Presidents, are you very fond of them?" I asked circumspectly.

"Oh, I served under them. They too were fond of me."

"In what capacity."

"I was ADC to the Rashtrapati from 1964 to 1972."

Then in a reflective mood:

"Radhakrishnan always used to be with a book. He was a philosopher, everybody knows. V.V. Giri used to make me run the whole day. And Zakir Hussain used to love gardening, like the Moghuls, you know."

From the mundanity of an unknown existence to the rarefied levels of Victoria Cross, the man had indeed travelled a long way. The photographs in the room represent his proudest moments receiving honours from army luminaries. In one he is shaking hands with none other than Field Marshal Manekshaw. Expectedly V.C. Saab carried on about his numerous gallant deeds. In between enjoying a ceremonial drink, I tried to take him back to the 'earlier days' he had commented upon. But like a true soldier he stayed clear of anything political and time and again went back to his exploits in the army.

On our way back we came to know about something which we should have known before we went to visit the man. The only road that runs through Ravang is named after its most illustrious son. It is called the Gonju Lama road.

# Highway Hiccups

Next morning we headed for Gangtok. The weather remained the same. The road was bad particularly at certain points between Singtam and Ranipool. Our journey was uncertain but nothing in comparison to the one we were to experience nearly 3 years later from Geizing to Siliguri. That was 15th August and only the previous afternoon we had learnt that the Pelling - Siliguri bus for the day had been cancelled as there were not enough passengers, and more importantly, as everyone would be busy in celebrations. That year being the 50th year of Indian independence festivities were more high key than usual. I had left my family with my in-laws at Jalpaiguri and we were to meet at the railway station and catch the evening train to Calcutta. I had planned to take the morning bus so that I would reach in time. That night as we returned to the PWD bungalow our driver gave us bad news. There had been a huge landslide at Teestabazar and the road to Siliguri was entirely blocked. Some people were making it by transshipment which too was very uncertain, he told us. I hardly slept that night.

Occasionally when I dozed off I dreamt of the winged horses that I found on the crockery in the bungalow. I dreamt that those horses would take me flying to my destination, rather than vehicles which could slip any moment to the ravines below. We managed a lift to Geizing next morning. At that early hour the town looked ghostly. Nothing on wheels was going to Siliguri we were told by a group of shop-workers busy in their morning chores. We waited in the light drizzle. School-children in bright uniform ran by to attend the celebrations. Trekkers full of football players headed for Pelling to participate in a local tournament. Patriotism however was the last thing on my mind then. The situation was grim. After about an hour a trekker full with passengers arrived. It was going to Siliguri.

"Could we make it ", I asked the driver, a pencil - thin man who didn't exude much confidence.

"We can at least try".

"But the road is blocked".

"Then we will try through Darjeeling", he said making a last-minute check on his vehicle.

"Jai Srikrishna", a Hindustani passenger chanted.

"No risk, no gain", he winked at us.

We jumped in at the behind and the journey began.

Occasionally we found buses and maruti cars and vans turning back. The road had become too narrow for the buses and too slippery for the latter. Our commander had better chance of making it. Up to Legship the journey was uneventful, nothing to cause concern. Thereafter the road got worse. There were frequent stoppages and vehicles were negotiating the muddy roads with the narrowest of margins. At every point of alarm the Hindustani raised his chant and as our vehicle overcame it he flashed a winning smile at the rest of us.

It was just before Jorethang that we had the scare of our lives. The metallic road just vanished. Ahead for about 20 meters it was a thick pool of mud and slush, slippery and treacherous. The landslide had taken away half of the road leaving a narrow path just about enough for a vehicle to squeeze through. Slip an inch or two and you are straight into the ravines thousands of feet below. Some labourers worked hard at firming up this path lest its softness give away to the pressure of the vehicle. A maruti stood aside on the other side of the mess. It had been turned back. Two more vehicles waited behind ours at a distance. We were the first to cross the stretch since the landslide occurred.

Our driver got down, inspected the path, enquired something from the labourers and walked back to the vehicle with brisk steps barking orders for everyone to get down and walk on foot to the other side. Everyone hurriedly embarked. They took off their shoes. Some walked across with their ankles deep in the slush. The Hindustani did likewise holding his chappals over his head and hitching up his dhoti in his right hand chanting 'Jai Srikrishna', 'Jai Srikrishna',

Being city people, we acted clever. Who is going to walk in that muck, that too bare-footed in this cold and rain? We hardly realized the danger of staying on in the vehicle. Moments later when realization dawned and we tried to get down, the driver, who was by now at the wheel, turned around and pointing his finger at us shouted, "stay put". Likewise he ordered the helper to get in at the rear. "We need some weight at the back", he muttered. We froze and he rolled the vehicle forward. At my back were the hills, deep below the ravines. I even ventured to look down. The tyres were precariously right at the edge of the path. A couple of inches away and we would fly into space. The driver looked straight, the wheel almost static and stiff in his hands. The vehicle gathered momentum, changed gears to negotiate a ridge, violently landed on the other side, made some more distance and screeched to a halt. The driver leapt down from his seat walked up to me and ordered, "cigarette". Like a robot I handed to him my pack. Inhaling deeply, he looked at me, mischief in his eyes : "*Kaisa laga*. How was it", his eyebrows danced.

His spirit lifted after this scary escape. As he

drove he whistled. The Hindustani man was unruffled as well. Occasionally he chided the driver, " *Arre,* driver*ji*, it's ok that you are singing but there is no song on this road." He got down at a crossing from where there is a road to Kalimpong. Flashing a winning smile he told us, " I have brought you this far and from here on it's up to the gods."

Evidently with his departure the gods left us. The news about the huge landslide at Teestabazar was true. Efforts were going on to clear the rubble through blasting. It only helped in obliterating the narrow trail by which people were walking over to the other side and tranship. We turned back and made a fresh journey via Jorebunglow in Darjeeling. After a harrowing journey of nearly 12 hours we just about reached Siliguri in time.

# Small is Beautiful

No such drama this time. We didn't even have to take a detour and reached Gangtok in the afternoon and checked into the MLA hostel. Gangtok, the village - capital of Alexandra David Neal, the slumbering mist-covered settlement that I had seen in 1981 - a town almost elusive, veiled and forbidding. Two memories remain of that visit. A visit to the palace where I found young men practicing archery. This remained my only visit to the place as later it became a restricted area and one had to acquire special permission to visit its premises. Archery competitions are even now held occasionally in the state. But sadly as with many other such distinct aspects of Sikkim, its popularity has waned and mass spectacles like soccer and even cricket has become the popular pastime of the youth. The more abiding memory, one which as with archery, is strikingly representative of what Gangtok was and is no longer, is the incessant chant of mantras and hymns that went on all through out the day at a house next door to from where I lived. In today's perspective it is a haunting reminder of what Sikkim was supposed to be - the promised land of Buddhism - rather than yet another churning pot of religions, castes and nationalities. Peeping through the window of my house I watched lamas seated under a shamiana and immersed in prayers in the accompaniments of pipes and cymbals. The cremation rites of a Bhutia gentleman was going on and later I learnt that it is an elaborate and extravagant process spanning all of 49 days. The dead body is kept at home for this entire period. It is smeared in indigenous herbs and covered in plastic and kept in a palanquin made of wood. It is placed in a sitting position and its decomposition smell is covered by incense which is made more smoky and fragrant by adding pine leaves. A host of lamas and lama boys do the puja. The number of lamas depend on the financial position of the deceased's family. They stay in the house for all these days and are paid for their services. Prayers start as early as 3 O'clock in the morning and continue till late into the night. People who drop in offer money to the family. On the other hand relatives of the bereaved go around monasteries in the vicinity offering puja and prayers. After 49 days the body is taken to the local monastery in a ceremonial procession. The palanquin is placed atop a pyre of 8 ft. height and put on fire. The lamas then return to the house with baskets full of stones. They close the doors and windows of the room in which the dead stayed and throw stones all around. Then in accompaniment of a musical band they march to the nearby hills thus exorcising the spirits which had been responsible for the death. A feast quite like the *shradh* ceremony of the Hindus follow a few days later where friends and relatives are treated to food and drinks. A Bhutia acquaintance told me that he had spent as much as 3 lakhs on one funeral ceremony. Considering the Bhutias are mostly well off, few grumble about the costs. But for the poorer ones death brings in its trail a heavy financial burden. To meet the costs, they borrow and get mired in a debt trap which take generations to overcome.

Gangtok in 1994 was vastly different from what I saw 13 years ago. As if the sleepy town of yore had evaporated or lost its way in the by-lanes of history. As if it had not existed at all and what I had seen was only a figment of imagination. That veil of elusiveness had been ripped apart and what stood out instead was just another Indian town, vapid and stereotyped.

Unfortunately a style of development suited to the plains has been mindlessly applied here resulting in ugly high-rises obliterating traditional architecture. The unbelievable spree in the building of high-rises has scarred the capital's skyline for good. Shaggy rods, crude pillars, antennas, concrete fronts make up the sky-scape today. Gone are the prayer flags, that ubiquitous symbol of Buddhism which flutter in the wind and spread the message of the great teacher far and wide.

It was in that year, during the state assembly elections that I had a dramatic introduction to Ram Chandra Poudyal. "I am R.C. Poudyal, president of the Rising Sun party", he walked up to me and said, vigorously shaking my hand. I had heard his name although for an entirely different reason. A few months ago he made news in Calcutta, may be in other parts of the country as well. He foretold doom. He predicted that a *mahapralay* would strike the earth on 16th May and life would cease to exist. It would cause the end of *kaliyug,* the age of evil and herald an era of peace and harmony, the *satyayug*. Newspapers lapped up the story; vernaculars in particular splashed it on their front pages and it did seem that life was indeed doomed. On that day many people didn't venture out. Attendance at schools and offices were low. Streets were emptier than usual. Many in fact closed doors and windows at their homes to keep the catastrophe away. Nothing of course happened but RC became quite a name in West Bengal.

The way he shook my hand knowingly and with a grin, I thought he would be speaking about that event. But pulling up his shirtsleeve and pointing to a deep gash on the back of his elbow he said:

"I am a man born twice".

Again I thought, well this man is cooking up another round of metaphysical rubbish.

"I was declared dead. The word spread that I was dead. People thought that I was dead, yet I came back alive". RC said with a mischievous smile.

He invited me to his house for lunch the next day and I heard the rest of the story there. His ancestral house is at Ranipool and his country house another 15 minutes drive from there at Asom Singtam. Through a muddy track, through terraced cultivated hills, I reached there. The house had the look of a rebel of the sixties : un-kept beard, long unwieldy locks, *jhola* by the side, chappals, and as it was in the west a guitar slung across. The house was likewise : unkept, long unwieldy weeds, cows loitering, a lonely garage with a lonely car and the freedom of having no definite boundaries. We sat on the roof in the comfort of a mellowed December sun and Gangtok glimmering hand-shaking distance away.

"I am always against monarchy, you know ", he began characteristically.

"I even went to Nepal to participate in the agitation there. My father fought against the former Chogyal Tashi Namgyal. He was a leading figure in the 1949 revolt".

Then he continued about that revolt. I unmindfully leafed through a hefty book of religion.

"Oh, that's Vedas, the greatest book of religion ever. Islam is nothing new. It's contained in this. Whatever the Muslims say is contained in this".

I turned away from the book. I had no time for religious sermons. I was more interested in that deep, awesome gash on his elbow.

"You were influenced by your father ?"

"Obviously. Everybody is. I was the president of the Sikkim Students Association in Darjeeling. Many of its members later formed the nucleus of the anti-Chogyal agitation."

Off and on a vehicle passed by that muddy track. Limboo and Lepcha peasants worked in the distant fields.

"I launched a hunger strike in 1972 in front of the palace. It shook the Chogyal"

An unknown bird whistled by. A gust of wind flattened the weeds. Mrs. Poudyal herself brought tea and snacks.

"After Sikkim became an associate state (September, 1974) Chogyal revealed his true colours. He knew that his days were numbered. He denigrated the assembly, he publicity humiliated the political leaders, he called us *Deshbechowas*. Then he got his opportunity when he was invited to the coronation ceremony in Nepal."

"I have read it in Das's book, The Sikkim Saga",

I told him.

"You have, but take it from me. There he blasted India at a press conference. He called the assembly a hoax and even met the Chinese delegation."

Later I heard other versions of that incident. "It's a cock-and-bull story", a political leader told me. "Chogyal was the most pro-Indian of all the Sikkimese". A person who was close to the royal family vehemently shook his head when I asked him about the incident. "Why would he do that? His family had a very warm relationship with Mrs. Gandhi's family. He never expected anything drastic from New Delhi. You know he was offered asylum by foreign embassies. But he flatly refused".

On his return we blocked his cavalcade at Rangpo. The people were incensed. It was a huge crowd and they wouldn't let Chogyal enter Sikkim".

I lit a cigarette and again absent -mindedly caressed that hefty book. Many of its pages were marked, many lines underlined with a variety of colours.

"Whatever I professed may not have happened", he said falteringly. I cursed myself for having distracted him again from the main story. I felt confronted by a strange man, a combination of a politician and a sadhu.

"Some day my predictions will come true".

R.C. had also given the exact time at which the

apocalypse would occur. He had also said that people who performed puja and *yagna* at that particular time (11am.3mints.48secs.) at which the mahapralay were to strike, would be saved. Indeed many people had gathered from the early hours of the morning at the gate of his house. They lit up fires, chanted mantras and invoked the almighty to save them from the disaster. They were under the belief that by being near R.C.'s house they would have an easy and direct passage to the satyayug. Later when the prediction turned out to be a hoax they demanded that R.C. be arrested and even put in the asylum.

We then went off for lunch. It was like RC and his house, a simple but satisfying affair. It was vegetarian with Mrs. R.C. serving. Saag, chupri, a mish-mash of curd and radish almost a local cheese, cauliflowers, chutni, it was a conglomeration of dishes. The utensils were clean, the kitchen spic and span, and the entire experience pure, shorn of all the extravagance and grandeur that mark such an invitation.

RC didn't allow me to smoke in the room where I rested after lunch. The effect was I dozed off. The story resumed only in the afternoon, again on the roof. The sun had gone down. A cool breeze blew across. The fields were empty. The cows had gone back to their sheds.

"We made a mistake you know. The Sikkim guards

were still under the control of the Chogyal".

I appreciated the man. Even in 1994, when some leading people had turned against the merger, when the illusion of being with India and reaping rich harvests had faded, when even pro-India veterans like Kazi and Khatiwada had denounced the merger and demanded restoration to the protectorate status, this man talked about the event without any remorse or repentance. With utmost conviction he still held the view that Sikkim's merger with India has only benefited the hilly state , brought much needed development to the area.

Such zeal and conviction is the prerogative of the true believer, I thought. No wonder that during a later visit RC expressed the opinion that fanaticism is good. I was appalled. The very word brings to my mind hoodlums climbing atop a centuries old mosque like monkeys and pulling it down.

He sensed the disbelief on my face. He was amused.

"Fanaticism can be both good and bad. Swami Vivekananda's fanaticism was good; Sangh Parivar's is bad". Silence.

"Swamiji devoted his entire life to the cause of Hinduism. Do you think that's easy? He could do it because his conviction was not shallow; it lay deep down in him, strong, no shadows of doubt or confusion whatsoever.

Fired by such fanaticism RC led the mob that gheraoed the Chogyal at Rangpo chowk.

"The Sikkim Guards went berserk. They charged left and right with their khukris. I do not remember how many chops I took nor do I remember anything that happened in the next few days. I came to know that I bled profusely and was flown to a military hospital. There the doctors thought I was dead, the word went round that I was dead. For few tantalizing moments they couldn't get my beat or pulse. Then I miraculously survived. I have been in that zone, you know, between life and death. Dark, dark, blinking .........." he gestured with his fingers, still looking amused.

Captain Yongda whom many people including ministers asked us to meet as he is known to be knowledgeable about the state, has a different version of the story. He was with the

Chogyal in his car. As they were entering Rangpo they found a car parked across the bridge. "R.C. Poudyal was standing on the bonnet and screaming we will not let you enter Sikkim." Imagine a small fry like him obstructing the king to enter his domain. I wanted to get out of the car and put an end to all this nonsense but the Chogyal restrained me. Suddenly there was pandemonium all around. People were jumping into the river crying, "man killed! man killed! " R.C. was by the side of our car in a flash showing his hand to the Chogyal which was bleeding. What could the Chogyal do about it! We had no idea as to who attacked him." Soon after their pilot car removed the obstacles and they proceeded to Gangtok without any further trouble.

This incident sparked off fresh agitations. On April 10, 1975 a referendum was held to decide Sikkim's merger with India. An overwhelming majority voted in favour of merger and Sikkim, which only two years ago was an independent country albeit as a protectorate, became the 22nd state of India. Many claim today that there was a lot of confusion as to what the referendum was for. Some thought it was a choice between democracy and monarchy, yet others a straight fight between L.D. Kazi and Chogyal. This is quite possible considering the quick time in which the referendum was arranged and also taking into account the widespread illiteracy that then prevailed in the state.

"I had nothing personal against the Chogyal", R.C. took a deep breath. "He came to this house. Even Gyalmo came. They wanted to send me abroad for higher studies."

"But do you have any idea what would have happened if we did not merge with India. We would not have survived. Look what has happened in Bhutan. Nepalis have become refugees there."

Darkness had descended. The cows had gone home. The peasants had gone home. Streetlights were on and Gangtok glittered at a distance. It was time to leave.

That trip in 1994 sowed the seeds of this book. It was an exciting time to be in Gangtok. Assembly elections were just over and all of Sikkim waited with bated breath about the results. The earlier elections, particularly the ones in 1979 and 1985, were mainly contested around the merger sentiment. Though merger itself never became an issue, simply because no party dared raise it, voting was along anti-merger and pro-merger lines. Nar Bahadur Bhandari who had gone to jail several times espousing Sikkim's independence spectacularly carried the anti-merger sentiments with him to win both the elections. During the former his party was not even a registered one and all his candidates won as independents. During the 1989 elections, though his popularity was considerably on the wane he managed to stave off an upbeat opposition with a combination of strong arm tactics and political cunning that had become the hallmark of his leadership. During all these battles he fought against an array of merger veterans, deshbechowas, people who sold away their country, as they were referred to as by many people led by R.C. Poudyal. R.C. didn't do badly in 1979 winning 11 of the

32 seats but gradually faded away not even able to retain his own seat in 1989.

In 1994 nobody gave his party a chance. He had become a discredited man following his writ petition in the Supreme Court in which he sought the abolition of the sangha seat and reduction of B.L. Seats. He became dubbed as a communal leader bluntly catering to Nepali sentiments although other leaders did much the same albeit with far greater political acumen.

His arch-rival Bhandari was much in the same shape. Barely six months before the election he was ousted from power. Engineering defections from the ruling party, Congress for the first time formed a government in the state. Generally such coups create a sympathy wave for the ousted, particularly when they are masterminded from Delhi resulting in anti-center feelings overriding every other concern. But not this time. Bhandari's popularity was in the decline. Charges of corruption had tainted his image. Increasing authoritarianism had alienated him from the people. Clearly his honeymoon with the masses was over. Opposition to the regime rose from within, from the ranks of his own party. Pawan Kumar Chamling, a close confidant of his, heading a core group of only 18 members raised the banner of revolt : the SDF was born. " We gave the party a name, symbol and flag and the people could not believe that there could be a party opposing Bhandari. Such was the terror created then", one of the core members told me.

Significantly merger this time took a back seat. Thanks to Bhandari's authoratarian ways 'Restoration of Democracy' was the new mantra and when Chamling blended this with dollops of Mandal Commission, the latest import from the mainland, promising hitherto unheard of privileges for the backward castes, the Nepali vote bank was for the first time severely split and the signs became ominous for Bhandari. And yet nobody could underestimate the 'Bhandari' factor. In 1984 when he was removed in similar fashion, through defection, he returned to power in style. In 1989 when every one thought his days were numbered he swept back to power winning all the 32 seats. Clearly one could only write him off at his own peril.

The tension in Gangtok was indeed palpable. Violent clashes had preceded the polls. Many activists remained underground, many had sought shelter in neighboring West Bengal and Nepal. There was unprecedented distrust and suspicion amongst the various communities. Bhandari himself made a famous quote to me : that he would go on sanyas if not returned to power. Sanchaman Limboo, the congress chief minister was uncertain about his prospects. SDF exuded quite confidence but its leader Chamling remained cocooned in his fortified house away in Namchi refusing to even appear before the press. It was then that I met Uttam. He stood for the RSP from Rumtek and he was confident of winning. But who was going to come to power Chamling or Bhandari? He shook his head, he wasn't too sure. Even then he was a party-hopper, many young men like him in Sikkim are. He had joined the SDF when the party was floated nearly two years ago. Amidst the chants and cheers of a wild crowd he had dramatically taken out his SSP identity card from his pocket, tore it into pieces and threw it to the wind. He was one of the few active members of the SDF then and carried a revolver with him for protection. But then ruling party's pressure got too much and he had to cool his heels in Nepal. He came back, laid low for months and then joined the RSP. "This man RC will do something for Sikkim", he told me.

Predictably the loss devastated him. The evening before I left both of us went out.together searching for liquor. Not a drop was available anywhere. The state had been declared dry for the duration of the results. Finally Uttam could manage a bottle of brandy from one of his friend's hotel. We talked late into the night in my room. There was despair in Uttam's voice but he wasn't giving up. He said that he would start planning meticulously from now. He would get into more social work, build up a base, use his brother's paper to increase his popularity.

"It 's easy to become a leader here, you know. Sikkim is a small state".

# Panglhabsol

Panglhabsol is the celebration of the unique place that mount Kanchenjungha has in Sikkimese Buddhism and its far-reaching impact on the evolution of the Sikkimese identity. It is symbolic of the man and nature relationship, a reminder that human spirit cannot thrive in isolation, that man is born into nature, that he has a symbiotic bonding with hills, trees and rivers, an occult and intricate inter-dependence the snapping of which can only lead to civilisation's demise. This Buddhist festival originated in Tibet and was introduced in Sikkim by the third Chogyal, Chakdor Namgyal. Literally ' Pang' means witness and ' lhabsol' means celebrations. Keeping the grand deity Kanchenjungha as witness people exalt at the hallowed recreation of tradition, rejoice at the triumph of good over evil. The imposing massif is invoked to provide protection; to guard the frontiers, to save the little state from outside onslaughts. Also to save the crops and as a lama put it to ensure that there is not much rain and there is not less rain, just enough to save the elaichi—meaning cardamom. This festival is also a historic occasion as it marks the signing of the Blood Brotherhood treaty between the Bhutias and Lepchas.

"Blood Brotherhood?" an elderly Bhutia had raised his eyebrows when I had asked him about it. "I have never understood what people mean by it."

The story goes that Khye Bumsa, the mythical ancestor of the Chogyals of Sikkim had travelled from Tibet and settled in Denzong, valley of rice, the ancient name of Sikkim. He was a legendary fighter and drove away many devils and evil spirits from Sikkim. He had married a princess but for many years the couple had no children. A revered lama advised Khye Bumsa to meet Thekong Tek, the Lepcha chief and seek his blessings. He scoured the state with his followers and finally met the holy man at Kabi, a hamlet which nestles on the way to north Sikkim. He presented gifts and respectfully begged for his wish to be fulfilled. Thekong Tek was pleased with his devotion and blessed him with three sons. Since then the day of this meeting is celebrated as the beginning of an era of brotherhood between the Bhutias and the Lepchas. Like all relationships this too has gone through its share of ups and downs; while Lepchas have mostly been at the receiving end, the Bhutias by virtue of being in power have appropriated most of the benefits. Lepchas had been subjected to so much of exploitation that nearly 200 years ago situation reached a flashpoint when a Lepcha king Gebu Achuk decided to fight back. He was a great warrior and mobilised his tribesmen into a fearsome unit. They defeated the Bhutias, Bhutanese,and Nepalis in many battles and freed many Lepcha territories. In one such battle his domination was such that the enemy was forced to plead for peace. Having achieved victory Lepchas went into a celebration spree —— feasting, drinking and merry-making. At night when they were all asleep enemy forces sneaked into their camp and killed the valiant king. It is said that soon after there was famine and a series of epidemics in the area. The word went around that though Gebu Achuk was dead, his spirit was doing all the damage. People realized their mistake and offered puja and prayers in repentance thus renewing age-old relationships including the brotherhood pledge with the Lepchas.

Whatever be the state of the blood brotherhood pledge, Panglhabsol continues to be a major festival in Sikkim though its celebrations are now confined to specific regions in the state. We were on our way to Ravang to attend the celebrations and sat at a café at Singtam. The latter is like a town of the plains: warm, dusty and densely populated. The town was agog not with the celebrations of Panglhabsol but Biswakarma puja. Mikes blared, huge pandals had come up everywhere and hordes of young men collected donations from waiting vehicles. Biswakarma is a minor god in the pantheon of Hindu deities. While Brahma is the almighty Creator, Biswakarma is the humble artisan. It is a puja celebrated by the labouring class ——— the factory workers, transport unions, rickshawallahs, small traders etc. Votaries of Hindutwa had once demanded that May Day which is observed as the labourers' day worldwide be scrapped and Biswakarma puja instead be celebrated as the day of the workers. Fortunately people are now wise enough to ignore such cheap gimmicks.

The lady at the counter of our café was excited about the programmes that were coming up." There will be function on three consecutive nights. Drama, songs, magic, caricature. Artists will come from Siliguri ,Nepal, Bhutan."

But what about Panglhabsol? Isn't it celebrated here? She pointed to the hills. " It happens there, on the top".

Lama Lhatsun Chhembo, the patron saint of Sikkim who converted the state to Buddhism would not have been pleased. In his beloved Sikkim the faith is now confined to north district and some areas in the south and west.

Our mood lifted when we boarded the trekker to Ravang. It was mobbed by a group of youth who were all going to attend the festival. Indeed this time there were twenty of us in the trekker with five teenagers making the journey standing on the rear door. We sat close to their legs. As the trekker moved up it began to get cold. The rain too played truant. One moment it was pouring with all the fury, the very next moment it was gone. When it poured three of the boys crawled underneath the roof. The other two somehow squeezed in their heads. They didn't bother about the lower halves of their body getting wet.

" Are you going to Ravang?" Suvendu asked one of the boys, who was hardly 17-18 and who in his rimless glasses and cropped hair looked like a character straight out of Bernardo Bertolucci's ' The Last Emperor'.

" Yes, to the festival", the boy said.

" You live at Ravang?"

" No at Gangtok. My school is at Ravang".

Suvendu looked puzzled.

" Why study in a school so far?"

" I didn't get chance at Gangtok", the boy murmured shyly.

There was an uneasy pause. The driver waved at a passerby. The boys continued their jostling at the rear door.

" You live in a boarding?"

" No as a paying guest." One of his friends called

out to him and the upper portion of his body vanished over the roof.

It was almost at the fag end of the journey that we realised that it was not only the periodic stoppages of rain that was enticing the boys to the top of the vehicle.

" Grass", Suvendu whispered.

I nodded and went off to sleep.

There was no monastery the last time we had visited the place. One has come up recently though it isn't fully complete. Earlier people of this town used to go to Ralong during the festival. This time the jubilation was all the more as they would be able to celebrate it at their own place. This being another feather in the cap for the SDF government the chief minister himself was coming to grace the occasion. Also with panchayat election just round the corner it provided an excellent opportunity to the party to reach out to the people. On the morning of the festival the sky was like a muddy pond and there was a nagging drizzle. It is believed that on this day the weather clears out enough for everyone to have a view of the revered peak Kanchenjungha. Even Kishoreda agreed that the day of the festival is usually a sunny one. Though there was no sign of that as yet, braving the weather everyone was headed for the monastery up on the hills. Many were in their traditional dress —— the men in *bakhu* and the women in *honju*.

The monastery was all decked up. There was a constant chiming of bells by revolving the colourful *thuji shimphu*. There were a variety of offerings placed in front of the idols which included *torma* which is made of rice balls. There were lamps all around and *dhup* made of milk, butter-cheese, rice, dal and sugar, which burns all day and gives out a sweet fragrance. Shamianas were put up and partitioned into separate enclosures. One for the VVIPs, one for local VIPS —— the hoteliers, school teachers, bank, post office, power complex employees ——— one for refreshment and one for press as well. Women were mainly clustered around the refreshment area where plates of *jero*, in north Indian parlance *chatpati*, made from rice and made in several designs, were served. Tea and coffee were also available.

We met D.D.Bhutia here. He was pleased with a travel piece of mine which had appeared in a Calcutta newspaper. He got us seated in the press enclosure. Finding that it was virtually empty and there was no one else to give us company we shifted to the local VIP enclosure. Soon the CM arrived closely followed by the VC saab who in his bowler hat looked like a pucca sahib. He waved to us and we waved back. We had made a cursory call on him. He had shown us a book on VC awardees in which there was a chapter on him. He had given us xeroxed copies of that chapter. In it Roy Gribble,

Gonju's officer had commented on the young soldier: " Gonju came into my dug-out at four o'clock the next morning with a mess-tin full of tea and just said 'get up'. No 'good morning', no 'Sir' or anything and I thought well, this chap is rather extraordinary..............My heart warmed to him and I thought, well I have got something here". The citation for the Victoria Cross gives a vivid description of the battle which brought him the award: " Rifleman Gonju Lama........................on his own initiative and great coolness and complete disregard for his own safety, crawled forward and then engaged the tanks single-handed. In spite of a broken left wrist and two other wounds, one in his right hand and one in his leg, caused by withering cross-fire concentrated on him, Gonju Lama succeeded in bringing his gun into action thirty yards of the enemy tanks and knocked out first one, then another; the third tank being destroyed by anti-tank guns. In spite of serious wounds he then moved forward and engaged with grenades the tank crews, who now attempted to escape. Not until he had killed or wounded them all, thus enabling his company to push forward, did he allow himself to be taken back to the regimental aid post to have his wounds dressed. Throughout this action Gonju Lama, although very seriously wounded, showed complete disregard for personal safety, outstanding devotion to duty and determination to destroy the enemy, which was an example and inspiration to all ranks." Even late in his life VC saab retains the same qualities and is distinguishing himself in various social work, including looking after schools and monasteries.

As the CM's entourage entered there was a scramble for the presentation of *khadas*, the ceremonial scarf. Then followed the speeches after which the warrior dance by the masked lamas began. All the while it drizzled persistently. Suvendu tried valiantly to take a few snaps but then, exasperated, withdrew under the shamiana. I helped myself to pots of coffee and watched the proceedings. Series of dancers appeared in the courtyard and then disappeared into the monastery. The sequence went on and on with a drum beating furiously and pipes and blow-horns blowing. Suvendu complained that he had seen a much better performance at Rumtek which is understandable because it is the Rumtek monastery which trains the lama-dancers and lays down the rules according to which the festival is observed. Later a local lama told me the monastery being a new one, the dancers were not well trained. Again due to fund shortage they had not been able to obtain the right costumes. Almost a year later I met Captain Yongda at the Pemayangtse monastery. Captain was harshly critical about the state of the monasteries. " There is a sangh MLA, there is also an ecclesiastical ministry. But there are little funds and no budgetary allocation. Monasteries have to survive on their own meagre resources."

However tardy the presentation the people lapped it all. With every defeat of the Evil they cheered lustily and when it all ended around noon, noisily walked back to the market square. The day had only begun. After lunch there would be a volleyball tournament followed by an award-presentation ceremony. The festivities would end with a cultural soiree which was expected to end late in the night. We had precious little to do and whiled away time in a room the owner of which was a Bengali. His pub was just opposite to where we sat and it was teeming with people eating and drinking.

"We call him Aurobindo Bhutia. Do you know why?" Duttada asked.

We assumed like Kishoreda he is just another Bengali entrepreneur.

" Actually he is Aurobindo Pal, from Siliguri. A few years back he came here with his friends on a picnic. He got a little too intimate with the *malkin* of that hotel. People forced him to marry her. She is almost twice her age and what's more, you know, she has a whole lot of children", Duttada burst out laughing.

Duttada has been at Ravang for almost three years. The SBI does brisk business in the area. Its advances are mainly into cardamom plantations and transport and the repayments in the latter segment is good. The bank also finances exotic activities like jhora-fishery. Duttada lives in a sprawling flat and has his meals at Mainam. Many teachers also have their meals here. There is no dearth of schools in Sikkim although, many of them are in poor shape. Beautiful, lively children trudging their way to school is one of the great sights on Sikkim's roads and highways. Because of the free uniforms and mid-day meals, many students even get admitted to more than one school. However standards have hardly improved despite the fact that the state boasts of one of the best student-teacher ratio in the country. There are 735 government schools in the state with 150306 students and teaching staff of 7771. The student-teacher ratio is 19:1 which is better than even many reputed private schools in the country. It is said that while the government schools in the capital fare relatively well in the school leaving exams, there are schools in the districts which at times don't have any students in the particular class because no one passed from the previous one the last year.

We spent the evening at Duttada's flat seeing TV and listening to music. I pulled his leg regarding his fascination over Rabindrasangeet.

" I am a heart patient. It soothes my heart, why do you grudge that"? he would say again and again.

Ravang goes to sleep around seven but that night

even at ten the streets were full with people. Everyone danced, hugged each other. Hindi songs were blaring from the make-shift stadium. Liquor flowed and the bars were full. Restaurants had run out of food. The entire day the drizzle hadn't stopped. The devout still maintained that the sky had cleared up enough for everyone to have a clear glimpse of the grand deity. People live in faith, people live in tradition. I caught hold of a local lama and asked him the meaning of Ravang. ' Ra' means goat and 'Vang' means to get wet. A place where goats get wet. A place of perennial rain.

# Old Town, New Friends

Uttam had once again changed tracks. From being a photographer, a model-photographer he had turned to travel-operating. His ground- floor room had metamorphosed into a travel outlet. The first time I saw it, it was a typing-cum-xerox shop managed by his younger brother. Thereafter Uttam had turned it into his studio. On an earlier visit he had shown us portfolios of some of his models. "Sikkimese girls are ready for bigger things, you see. They can now even walk the ramps in Bombay or Delhi." We nodded. At that time he would be busy hunting opportunities for his models, getting them hooked to some agency or other————never mind if he himself got hooked sometimes. Within a year he shifted and here he was running a travel agency. " I am not giving up photography. It has always been my hobby ever since my father gifted me a camera in my school days." The room now announced exotic treks ———— Dzongri, Gochala, Mainam ———and monastic tours. "Get me some Bengali tourists. Should I give an ad in *Bhraman*. If I can catch the Bengalis and foreigners, I will make it", he raised his arms in triumph. "There is more money in this line. Foreigners *pakro*, pounds and dollars, dollars and pounds", he chuckled. Then with mischief in his eyes: "if you are lucky enough you will come across the odd lady traveller, lost and lonely, to whom you have to lend a helping hand on the tough climb of Gochala, pitch her tents and even warm her sleeping-bags ",he would break into peels of laughter. " There was a lady, French or German, I don't exactly remember. Arre yaar, she would not leave me after we came back to Gangtok. I had a harrowing time shaking her off. If somehow my wife came to know.................."

Remembering how he was determined to succeed in politics I would often ask him about his political plans. He would retort: " Tell me am I cut out for politics."

" No, not at all", I would shake my head vehemently. I always thought he had it in him to make it as a photographer; publish coffee-tablers, get into ads, print greeting-cards.

" I have friends in political parties. I have friends in the government. I can always get my work done through them. Why do I need to get into politics."

The matter would rest there.

The lure of politics is real. In a small place where there are few jobs available where business opportunities are limited, for bright young men, particularly of the elite, *rajniti* is the way to name and fame. And the icing on the cake is the enormous prospect of making money, and lots of it. Unfortunately, like the rest of the country, the culture of corruption has become ingrained in the political system. Before every election hordes of young men flock to political parties. They bring with them finance, they pawn whatever they have earned. They know if they end up on the winning side they could recover whatever they have spent and ensure themselves an income which is unimaginable in any other sphere of life. If they end up on the losing side, they drift away like shifting sands, get into some business or other and wait for the next opportunity to come along.

Even older men like Rinchen Wangdi, who is respectfully referred to as Yabla, fall prey to this lure. After the eclipse of the Namgyal regime he remained under house arrest for months and then went away to Bombay seeking fortune in Bollywood.

" You wanted to become another Danny?"

"I had gone to Bombay on compulsion. I had no ambition to become an actor."

He worked with Sakti Samanta, a film director in Bombay in roles which he described as 'glorified extras'.

Uttam had introduced us to Yabla. I also came to know that I could ask him about Chogyal's family if I wanted to. When I met him for the first time at his home in downtown Tadong, he queried, " what do you require of incompetent, insufficient Sikkim?"

He is a frail man who walks with a limpish gait. He was dressed impeccably, wore a scarf and occasionally cleared his nose.

Knowing that I had nothing to answer he continued: " Outside people are dominating us. Most of the buildings in Gangtok belong to outsiders."

" Yes it is painful to see Biharis and Marwaris monopolising trading", Suvendu remarked.

" Not only that, now Bengalis are taking up all hotels", Uttam retorted.

It's true. Bengalis are taking hotels on lease and importing their staff from their native districts. Hotels are a big source of employment in Sikkim and if this trend continues soon there will be no employment for the locals.

" Only people who are Sikkim Subjects should be allowed to do business here", remarked Yabla.

A Register of Sikkim Subjects was drawn up in 1961 on the basis of which electoral rolls were revised in 1973. The assembly election in 1974 was held on the basis of these electoral rolls. Later many outsiders, some put the figure at more than a lakh, got themselves listed in the voters list even though they were not registered subjects of Sikkim. Important political leaders even alleged that the Regulation on Sikkim Subjects be scrapped as it was doctored to favour the BL community as against the Sikkimese Nepalis. However, the fact is that the latter form almost seventy percent of the Register. It remains a controversial issue, a political football as it were. Ideally no one other than a Sikkim Subject can own property in the state.

" Outside people are much smarter than us. We have remained backward. Our terrain is such that we cannot use tractors, HYV seeds. Modern agriculture has bypassed us."

Chinese lanterns, Buddhist thankas, artificial flowers and a bust of Elizabeth, the sit-out where we talked was simply decorated. Uttam had brought along two of his friends ——

Norzeng and Kiran. Norzeng is a big man with a roaring laughter, a very happy-go-lucky person. I had met Kiran earlier in 1994 when he was the BJP candidate from the Gangtok constituency. All of them held Yabla in high esteem. People had told us that he is a rich man but we found that he does not believe in flaunting his riches. He used to be a contractor by profession and was involved with the Rathong Chu project and also the power project at Legship. I asked him about the former.

" They should not have started it. Once started

they should not have stopped it."

His observation was typically political. Contrary to what he said, the scrapping of the project earned the SDF regime enormous goodwill, particularly among the Buddhist community and environmentalists, so much so that Chamling was nominated as the Green CM by a Delhi-based magazine 'Down To Earth'. Captain Yongda even told us that, after the project was withdrawn, at several monasteries monks vowed not to support any leader other than Chamling in the future.

"Did you know Hopecook Namgyal?" I was itching to ask Yabla this question all evening.

" What about that? Why suddenly you want to know about her?" Yabla asked with a mischievous smile." She is history. Nobody remembers her any more."

In the 1970s and even later India was paranoid about the West. Every domestic crisis was linked to the so called 'foreign hand'. A white man on the street was either a hippie or a CIA agent, a white woman the very epitome of evil.

" People say that it was her presence in the palace, her strident anti-India postures, her efforts to distance Sikkim from India, which finally led to the degeneration of the relationship between the two neighbours."

" I can't judge. All I can say is that she was a complete misfit in our society. She was like today's teenagers ——— shallow," Yabla said with that smile still hanging on his lips.

Captain Yongda told me that he was terrified of being in the lady's presence as he could not comprehend a single word of what she said, so typical was her pronunciation. On one of my visits to the 'Institute of Tibetology' in Gangtok a veteran scholar, who has spent a lifetime in studying Tibetan Buddhism and who has been in Sikkim for more than 30 years, whispered in my ear: "She had formed a secret society like there was in China. She was the queen bee. She wanted be like Mao-Ze-Dong's wife ———— what's her name?"

" Now that you have racked up an old issue, tell me what you feel about Sikkim's merger with India", Yabla asked.

"So you have now passed the ball in my court", I feigned helplessness and there were smiles all around.

" At least I think that we all agree on one point. That it's better to be with India than with uncle China", Yabla said and everyone burst out laughing.

Later we rode his Toyota to Tibet hotel where he treated us to dinner. During my first trip I had stayed here for several days and if one is looking for the ethnic touch this is the hotel to be in Gangtok. There is Tibetan music, a separate Tibetan cuisine, and there is the burly durwan who with his pin-hole eyes, divided-at-the-nostril and drooping, unruly moustache, patang hanging at the waist and skull cap, is a character straight out of Kublai Khan or Tamur Long's days. Suvendu had never had a better photo opportunity. With every click he made the burly man would break into a rapturous smile and bow elaborately in gratitude. There were more bows as we entered the hotel. The ladies at the reception stood up, waiters scurried to help us with our chairs, a middle-aged steward ushered in Yabla. The man is obviously widely respected.

" But why suddenly in politics", I asked as I savoured the excellent chilli pork.

" Because I want to serve my people."

Besides us the restaurant was virtually empty. Here in the lobby I had interviewed several politicians including Kiran Chhetri who now sat beside me nibbling vegetables. Kiran has an interesting past. In 1985 he along with some others had sneaked into Nepal where they approached several embassies pleading their help for the de-merger of Sikkim. They obviously found support from Pakistan. Kiran came back to Gangtok and announced the same at a press conference. He was promptly arrested under National Security Act and packed off to Berhampore jail. Later he formed the Naya Sikkim party which demanded de-merger. In 1994 he joined BJP which predictably made little impact in Sikkim. He then became a floater, joining one party or the other.

" We want to preserve our culture and tradition", Yabla continued. " I think this can be done better if I am in politics."

" I consulted the lamas of Pemayangtse monastery before I took the decision."

" How did they react?" I asked.

" They were reluctant, they said I am not fit for politics. Finally they relented."

" Is it the custom to consult the lamas before every such major decision?"

" We usually do, at least I do. I am very close to them. It depends from person to person."

It was well past midnight when we left Tibet hotel. The streets were deserted barring the occasional dog or a stray policeman doing the rounds. Late night Gangtok was not new to us. There had been occasions when we have been mobbed by friendly young men who have offered to take us to Chhangoo lake the following morning or beseeched us to promote their travel agency in Calcutta. We have met disgruntled Bihari traders closing shop after a hard day's work. They were furious about the Sikkim Subjects provision." Tell me where in India will you find a similar provision? Do you have a Bengal Subjects in your state? Or is there anything called Bihar Subjects in my state? And these people are always telling us to get out because we are not Sikkim Subjects." But then Sikkim is not like any other Indian state, we argued. It was a kingdom which has been incorporated with the Indian Union with the specific promise to preserve its distinct identity. Obviously our arguments made little impression on them and they dismissed us as tourists out to have some late night fun. On one occasion we had ventured out looking for liquor. Every town wherever it may be located has its joints where liquor is available any time of the day. We went to a shady restaurant which had already downed shutters and everyone had gone to sleep. After much knocking and shouting finally a sturdy, tough-looking lady emerged. As expected the lady was in a foul mood and demanded a phenomenal price for a pint. We had no option but to agree and as the lady was handing over the liquor to us Suvendu fished out his camera and clicked. All hell broke loose. The lady was livid and she was joined by her mother and their shrill voices created threatening echoes in the stillness of the night. We had a real battle on our hands. They snatched at Suvendu's camera and demanded that at least the rolls be handed over to them. It was only the presence of our local friends that saved the day for us.

# Across the Rangit

Rapid and reckless urbanization was taking its toll on Gangtok. Few were really surprised when landslides rocked the city and caused the collapse of several buildings in the Development area. Authorities sat up and made house building laws more stringent. The use of plastic bags was also banned through out the state. The capital now extends up to Deorali and may soon proliferate right up-to Ranipool, nearly 12 kms from the town. Roads are clogged with traffic. Some are one-way during peak hours. Traffic week is observed as it is in Calcutta. Masks are worn to ward off pollution. School children are drafted in to help the police. To take the pressure off Gangtok, the construction of a second city was announced. A consultancy firm was roped in to do the ground work on the project. Winters are now much warmer and old Gangtokians become nostalgic recalling earlier days when the season was much colder with persistent drizzles. Sikkim's old towns like Geizing and Mangan, the headquarters of West and North districts have suffered less from this ugly urbanisation spree. They remain, as of yore, trading centres where the occasional tourist stops by only to take a breather. There are fewer hotels in these towns, mostly dank and inadequate, catering to locals and traders. Tourism has bypassed them benefiting Chungthang, Lachen and Lachung in the north and Pelling in the West. Pelling is a classic case of how tourism can change the face of a place within a span of few years. Until the late eighties hardly anyone had heard about the place when it was an obscure village with only a tea shop, a grocery and a school which had been built by the Late Chogyal as the one at Geizing, then Gyalshing, was too far for the local children. Suddenly a bunch of students from Calcutta discovered that the place provides a spectacular view of Kanchenjungha. Add to it the village's proximity to Pemayangtse monastery and a PWD bungalow which hangs nonchalantly at the edge of a cliff. News of the beauty of a place spreads as fast as that of the beauty of a woman and, soon as if by magic, Pelling became everyone's destination.

We managed to squeeze out a booking in that bungalow and one dark, rain-threatened morning headed for the west. It was 10th of August and celebration of 50 years of Indian independence was well and truly on. Ministers were busy arranging artists for the finale in Delhi; photo exhibitions, cultural programmes and soccer tournaments were being held through out the state. During our journey we often came across trucks full of young boys travelling to and fro from football matches. Screaming themselves hoarse and egging on the driver to press on the accelerator they made a mockery of the highway warnings, ‘ Be late rather than The Late’ or ‘On my curves keep your nerves’. In between there were mini buses which were on a different journey ——— on a pilgrimage to Deoghar to keep their tryst with *bombhol*, meaning *bholebaba* or *baba Taraknath*, the post-modernist reincarnation of Lord Shiva. A visit to that holy place changes one’s life, our driver told us. He himself had been on such a pilgrimage after which he had turned into a vegetarian.

It is in the west that one first comes across Rangit, considered the other half of Teesta. In folklore Rangit is indeed the husband. It is said that up on the mountains the duo decided on having a race as to which could reach the plains first. Teesta chose a snake as its guide while Rangit chose a bird. The snake took the straight path guiding Teesta fast into the plains while the bird played naughty picking up a morsel here another there, calling on its mates, resting, gossiping and inevitably delaying Rangit’s journey. Ashamed at having lost the race to his wife, Rangit vent its fury by causing widespread floods in the plains.

One could not really blame the bird for straying

from the straight path and indulging itself in leisure and luxury. Sitting at a shop in Legship I felt like doing the same. Legship is the gateway to the west and it has benefited from the development around it. It has developed as a business centre and caters to Rangitnagar, the National Hydro Power Corporation township, close by. Otherwise life is almost a casual affair here. Children here roll on the grass rather than go to school. Women forget the drudgery of daily work, nitpick each other's hair and break into intriguing laughter as foreign tourists jostle for a shoot. Young boys juggle with a ball on the road. Rain can enliven such picture-perfect surroundings, rain can play a spoilsport as well. Clouds had chased us right from Gangtok and it is here that the first drops began to fall. It soon grew into a steady drizzle sending the women and children scurrying into their huts. The tourists ran back to their car, the revving up its engine merging with the rumble of the clouds. We remained where we were enthralled by the sudden change in the scenario.

It was rain and shine alternatively for the rest of our journey. A mile before Pelling our car turned right, worked up a gradient and screeched to a halt on the graveled courtyard adjoining a bungalow. It was locked and there was no one in sight. Side by was a hotel where two masons were working. As it was off-season the hotel was empty and there was no food and not even drinking water. The masons told us that Nima, the chowkidar lives down below. " Call out by his name and he will come up if he is at home." Walking over to the edge we called out as we had been told to. I shouted, Nima, Nima and Suvendu shouted, Nima, Nima; the hills replied Nima, Nima. This went on for quite some time and there was no sign of Nima. Taking matters into his own hands, our driver acted. Like a squirrel he danced down the messy slope into the gorge and vanished behind the thickets. Time passed. The drizzle came back. Swirling pools of mist rose from the ravines and created doodles in the sky. Tall unknown trees swayed in the air. The whack of masonery reverberated in the hills. I looked down into the gorge, the thickets beyond which was darkness.

At last we heard people talking and our driver accompanied by a lanky young man emerged from the bushes. He was in slippers and wore a long gown which served as a raincoat as well. He had a cap on, the flaps of which hung limply behind his ears. Everything about him was meek except his eyes which were like those of a trapped deer, restless, naughty and endlessly on the move.

" So Nima what are you giving us for lunch", I asked after we had settled into the warmth of the bungalow.

" Chicken *busti se*. Fresh. Provisions, we will have to fetch from Geizing."

" As it is I will have to go to the district office to get your bookings registered."

We too purchased some essentials at Geizing. I wanted to photocopy some documents but there was no electricity. Nima was doing the provisions and he also had to go to that office. With ample time on our hands we entered a hotel the name of which was well...........No Name.

" Hotel NO Name! Isn't that terrific ma'am?"

My question was addressed to a middle-aged, governess-like lady who was engrossed in intricate wool-work.

" Yes, it is", she smiled silently and then having cast a look on us continued: " We hadn't decided on a name the day we launched the hotel. A sahib was standing outside and suggested why not name it 'No Name'. And so it remained."

How the sahibs have left their mark everywhere. How often they have decided even small little things in the sub-continent.

We were famished and helped ourselves to pork momos which were boiled and rubbery and the stuffing under-prepared. In front of the hotel is a huge square which is the bus terminus. Geizing is an important junction and buses and trekkers ply from here to various parts of Sikkim. At the opposite end there are minarets jutting into the sky.

" You have a Muslim population here?"

" A few families. They are into tailoring and driving. In my childhood there was only one, selling biscuits."

During the Chogyal's time Muslims were not allowed to settle in Sikkim barring a handful of notable exceptions. They could however hawk their wares in various markets but were not allowed to stay there overnight.

There were several calendars on the walls: one of Dalai Lama and others of Hindu gods and goddesses——Laxmi, Parvati, Shiva, Ganesh the entire range. There was also a photograph of Sai Baba who seems to be quite popular in Sikkim. In between her knitting madam shouted orders to her boys, collected the bills besides of course chatting with the customers. Looking at her an old feeling came back to me: that women of Sikkim are more active than the men. Singtam, Mangan, Ravang, Legship, Geizing; everywhere it is the women who run the hotels and restaurants and men are nowhere to be seen. Does the Teesta-Rangit story actually reflect the reality of the Sikkimese society where the husbands are wayward and the women with their hard work keep the family going?

" Na, Na", madam vigorously shook her head.

" I am here because my husband is into some other work. It's as simple as that", she exclaimed. " He is a government contractor and obviously cannot spare time for the hotel. I have two daughters studying at Pondicherry and Gangtok. We need a healthy income to support the family."

" Is that true of everyone, ma'am?"

She paused for some time.

" I don't know. I can only say for myself."
She went back to her knitting.

At hotel Garuda in Pelling it was however Tshering Wangdi himself who was at the reception. At this hotel there is a clear division of work between the husband and wife duo. While Wangdi mainly looks after lodging and the bills, his wife Sumitra manages the kitchen and takes the orders. Garuda is a typically Hindu name, I thought: the mythical man-bird, the carrier of Indra, the king of heaven.

" But Garuda is also a part of Buddhist religion", Wangdi said. " It is one of the five sources of energy by harnessing of which a man can achieve his goal."

Garuda is the oldest hotel at Pelling and it has a distinct flavour of its own. The interiors have an ethnic feel. There are Chinese characters painted on the walls; tapestries, wall-hangings, lanterns and a cream colored scarf tied to the main pillar. There are buntings of Teem,

7up, Pepsi making one wonder as to who would be interested in so many varieties of cold drinks in so cold a place. There is a wide-angled photograph of the *Kalachakra* at Bodhgaya and the ambience summed up with an appropriate poster: " Honor Diversity. Stop Hate Crimes."

A few foreigners were hanging around: some glued to the BBC on a black-and-white TV, one engrossed in a book and a couple lost in themselves. Over the years travel restrictions in Sikkim has eased and now foreigners can visit even Lachen and Lachung in the north. However they are not permitted to stay for more than 30 days at a stretch. Various organizations in west and south Sikkim have been making repeated pleas to the government to lift this restriction as well, as it will enable the foreigners to take up exotic treks and carry out monastic studies in the area's famed monasteries. This will bring in foreign exchange and would be a great boost to tourism and also the local economy. They have.argued that since these two districts do not share border with China and as there are no army deployments here, lifting of the restriction will in no way jeopardize national security.

Suddenly lights went out. There was a solitary candle at my table which I lighted and then bending sideways asked: " Is there load-shedding in your country?"

The person was puzzled. “ Pardon”, he murmured.

“ Do lights go off in your country?”

“ Never heard of it”, he quipped.

“ Where from are you?”

“ Spain.”

“ Barcelona?” There was a distinctive rhythm in the way I pronounced it. Years ago watching Satyajit Ray’s ‘ Charulata’ I had similarly said aloud———— Medi—terre—ne—an————to which the entire audience had looked back in a way which had me scurrying for cover.

“ Picasso, Lorca, Bunuel!” I reeled off a least of Spanish greats.

“ Cartier-Bresson”, Suvendu chipped in.

The names hardly had any effect on the Spanish. I had a brain-wave and almost screamed——— “Rivaldo.”

“ Yes Rivaldo, great player. Barca! Barca!” Wangdi joined us after some time. There were now more candles on every table. The couple was more intimate: the lady rested her head on her companion’s shoulder.

“ Development has been quite hectic in Pelling.”

“ Yes, in 1994 there were only 6 hotels and now there are 34.”

However all of them were concentrated in a stretch of barely half a kilometer making the tiny getaway cramped and congested. I asked him about it.

" There is no harm in hotels coming up but yes they must be spread out", he opined. Incidentally he is also the secretary of the ' Pelling Tourism Development Association'.

There are also other dangers in such rapid development. Hotels come up indiscriminately. There is no soil test, no sanctioned plan, and masons dictate. It wouldn't be a surprise if in the future Pelling too has landslides as in Gangtok.

" Actually tourism should have two aspects ——— one will look after tourism and the other the administrative side. We can also hire a consultancy service which will suggest which places we can promote."

There was sound of heavy rain. The couple was now into drinks. The Barca man retired asking for his dinner to be served in his room.

" And what about the government, is it doing well?"

" Quite well, indeed. There has been considerable work in the villages."

Now electricity up to two points at villages is free. Water connection is also free and people no longer have to fetch water from the jhoras in bamboo cones as they used to do in earlier days. Free loans of Rs 20000 was also doled out for house building. Such benevolence with only 18 months to go for the election will surely serve the government well, I thought. Earlier for the first time ever panchayat elections were held in the state. SDF had a cakewalk as SSP boycotted the election demanding party-less panchayats. However it is to the Chamling government's credit that it has been able to decentralize democracy in Sikkim while major states like Bihar has still not been able to do it.

Wangdi arranged a car to drop us at the bungalow. Before we left we bought a few candles and had a candlelit dinner. The dining place is small but the cutlery and crockery are vintage on each of which is engraved the winged horses, the emblem of the Sikkim government, earlier of the Sikkim Durbar. It was a windy night with glass-panes clattering and chilly wind seeping through making the light whimsical and varying in intensity. At times it would be dim and then again bright, shortening and lengthening the shadows it cast on the walls. It was an eerie dinner supervised by an equally eerie Nima, ear-flaps up, gown dangling, his shadow looming octopus-like over the table. People say this bungalow was once upon a time the meditation centre of a revered Buddhist saint, Neljor Pema Chenchyug. It was during his time that the British institutionalized the system of Kazis, landed gentry who came to wield enormous power in the little kingdom. The saint along with the then Chogyal objected to this as they felt that it would divide the Sikkimese society. The British in those times were in no mood to heed to such trifles and punished the lama for his intransigence by evicting him from the place and turning it into a dakbungalow. It is said that the soul of Neljor Pema stalks the bungalow even today: the odd sound, the ominous creeks and croaks, the gurgle in the commode, the hoarseness emanating from the waterpipes. I have never believed in ghosts but such myriad sounds, the howling wind outside, the candle playing phantom on the walls, the snoring of my companion already deep into sleep and the sheer isolation of the place could shake even the most materialist of men. Often I sat up in alarm, checked into the bathroom to find out if everything was ok, peeped into the darkness outside and then lit another candle, perhaps to defend myself against any intruding spirit.

Ghosts and spirits are part and parcel of religion in Sikkim. The presence of the Evil or *Mahakal* is an integral part of Sikkimese Buddhism. This is mainly due to the early influence of tantric cults and also because Sikkim's indigenous people were, and many still are, nature worshippers. Most consider Sikkimese Buddhism to be only an extension of Tibetan Buddhism. While that is true in terms of the religious texts, the existence of locals demons and dakinis, ghosts and spirits provide

Sikkimese Buddhism a distinct identity of its own. To tame such local demons one needs to appease the local deities for which again there are specialised lamas at every monastery. Even today in the interiors many ailments are said to be caused by local spirits in which case the only cure is to invoke the local deities.

Early next morning we walked over to the Pemayangtse monastery and met Captain Yongda. We asked him if ghosts still exist in Sikkim.

" At one time there were various kinds of devils and spirits. But Chaktha Rimpoche, a powerful monk, drove all ghosts out of Sikkim. He used to live naked with only a tiger skin around his loins and with 40 kilos of iron chain dangling around his neck. He could levitate, you know. He could fly four inches above the ground."

" But people still believe in spirits. It is a part of our religion."

We were talking at his prayer room which was quite dark. He sat on mats, silhouetted in the early morning light, eating out of a wooden tumbler.

" Wooden containers are good for food. They don't contaminate", he smiled and then enquired if we had our breakfast.

The darkness in the room hurt the eyes and it took me quite an effort to make out his features. Captain is quite a name in recent Sikkim history. He was the ADC to the Chogyal during the time of the merger. He was his closest companion during that fateful trip to Kathmandu. Twice he went to jail espousing Sikkim's independence. During his second incarceration he was transferred to Darjeeling on health ground. It was in the mid-eighties and from within his cell in the district hospital he felt the full blast of the Gorkhaland agitation which was then at its peak. Violence does not suit us, he told us. It frustrates, it defiles our soul. It is an end without any end. A much chastened man, he is today a soldier turned monk; one who has given up his fatigues, his patang and taken up the ochre habits and rosary beads, one who has turned his back on the heroics of battle and set his gaze on the horizon of peace, one who talks of soul rather than the body, of permanent independence rather than temporary, one who talks of dharma.

" People told us that you know a lot about Sikkim."

" I know nothing about Sikkim. I only know about Pemayangtse monastery", he promptly corrected me.

" Our monasteries have no funds. We receive little help from the government. We have to manage with our own resources."

He kept aside the tumbler and drank from a brass container. Suvendu who was taking photographs of the monastery joined us in the room.

" Write about my school. I need help. I am trying to give education to orphaned and destitute children. The government must help me."

The name of the school is ' Denjong Padma Choeling Academy' and it was established in 1980. Its aim is to provide free education, boarding and other necessities of life for the orphaned, destitute and disadvantaged children of Sikkim. However for long the development of the school has been thwarted due to a chronic lack of funds.

" Isn't that the Dalai Lama?" I asked pointing to a photograph on a shelf. There was a row of shelves with a host of photographs, of dakinis and deities, leaders and saints.

" Yes, and can you recognize the young man beside him."

I got up and had a closer look at the photograph. It was the captain in his younger days.

" In 1980 he came to Sikkim to offer prayers at the Khandusang Phuk cave. I accompanied His Holiness during the trip."

He was also acquainted with the 16$^{th}$ Karmapa who used to hold prayers in the palace ground for Sikkim's well being. I asked him about the controversy over his successor. There were already two claimants to the title of the 17$^{th}$ Karmapa and a third popped up in north Sikkim later. Yabla had told us that if His Holiness Dalai Lama says that a stone is the Karmapa then everyone will accept that. But we came across lamas who are unwilling to take the Dalai Lama's word for it as he belongs to the Gelugpa sect and not the Kagyu sect of which the Karmapa is the leader. Captain also held similar views.

" Are there still monks who meditate in the high caves? Are there incarnates?"

" Surely why not. A 7-year old incarnate was spotted in a village 3 kms from here."

" Where is he now?"

" Nobody knows. Must be meditating in some high cave."

" What about the general standard of the monks?"

" Unfortunately that has declined. Most of them are illiterate."

" But it is said earlier even illiterate monks had in them age-old wisdom, could perform incredible feats."

" Some old monks have it still. A 92-year old monk who died just recently knew the secret of making herbal tea in the Sikkimese way. I wonder if with his death that tradition will now vanish."

Earlier local people used to barter herbal tea for silk and brocade from the Chinese. The latter was of high quality and was used towards making prayer flags and thankas.

" My feeling is that monks should have both monastic and modern education. I was brought up in that way. My father himself was a good practitioner. I used to study at the Geizing school and during vacations went to the monastery to study the monastic way of life. It was the same when I studied in a college in Darjeeling. But now monks don't want to go for modern education. They feel that it will pollute them, attract them to worldly living, distract them from the path of social and religious service. I am not able to change their thinking."

Other people did not quite agree with the idea of both types of education going hand in hand. They said that if that is the case then the monks will end up having no education at all.

" Actually times have changed and we must recognize that. Take for instance the idea of Renunciation. A century ago it used to mean turning your back on the world and strive in the search of Nirvana. It cannot be the same today. I am a Buddhist by faith but I have a family and I have to run my hotel. When I go to the market I find chickens being slaughtered and I can't help it. Actually I am only trying to be a Buddhist. I am only in the process of reducing my attachment to all the worldly things around me", Wangdi said passionately.

" There may be some exceptions but you cannot expect to find the same kind of monks as there were say, a century ago."

" Like the monks that have been described in this book", saying which he showed us that fascinating book, 'Magic and Mystery in Tibet' by Alexandra David Neal.

He has a small collection of books ———— fiction, travelogues, thrillers, heady treatises on Tibetan Buddhism ———— for the benefit of his lodgers, an aspect which is unique in any hotel that I have stayed in Sikkim.

We had just returned from watching a football match at the Pelling ground. It was so similar to the plains with crowd cheering their favourite team and some of them milling around the snacks-sellers, the *chanachurwala* and *badamwala* and even a *momowala*, selling stale vegetable momos from an aluminum container. I wondered if the celebrations around 50 years of Indian independence was for real. Even in Calcutta we hadn't found such enthusiasm.

" It is real. We have benefited hugely from the merger", Wangdi had no doubt.

" Look at Pelling, what it was and what it is now. The ground on which the match was played was a muddy lake. Now helicopters land there."

" Earlier life was hard, now money is flowing.

There are so many opportunities. Hotels, restaurants, transport, driving, portery, dalali, ticket-bookings."

He fell silent.

" Actually India is very close culturally", he said wistfully. He then walked away abruptly and returned soon with David-Neal's book.

" Keep this", he wrote my name on the book and handed it over to me. I was touched and began to leaf through its pages.

"Even the attack on Tibet is an attack on Indian civilization", he was quite emotional.

I didn't quite understand.

" Everything of Tibet originates from India. All the Buddhist sects had their roots in India. Most of our root-gurus were from India."

" But the 'Save Tibet' movement seems to be going nowhere. Governments all over the world are turning their backs on the issue."

" China will break up like USSR did. It too has many provinces, many peoples, many religions. It will collapse under our peaceful methods."

He excused himself and went away to attend to certain chores. It was twilight. Some light was filtering through the glass windows. Discussion on the match was going on at a nearby table. Some were having a quick drink before going home.

When he came back I asked him about Sikkim.

The government is doing well, but what about the society.

" It is now a fragmented society. Everybody has become conscious of his caste, sub-caste identity. Now BLs are tribes, Rais, Subbas, Gurungs are OBCs, Chhetris are Brahmins, goldsmiths and locksmiths are scheduled castes. There is complete distrust among various communities. Forward castes are becoming backward, Brahmins are becoming increasingly frustrated because of lack of opportunities."

The north Indian scenario is being repeated in Sikkim. The tiny state has landed itself into the same caste cauldron due to the implementation of the Mondal Commission's report. Like in other states the caste one is born into rather than merit has become the password to success. Caste based reservations in employment, in admission to schools and colleges have raked up unforeseen schisms in the society. These divisions further threaten to marginalize Sikkim's indigenous population. Many BLs feel insulted to be categorized as tribes. "Tell me, are we like Santals and Mundas that we will be called as tribes? We are BLs, a distinct category." Another section which feels left out all together are the Limbus. Along with the Lepchas they are considered to be the original inhabitants of Sikkim.

The state had a mixed population of Bhutia (Lhori), Lepcha (Menri), Limbu (Tsong) people, locally referred to as ' Lho Men Tsong Sum'. Indeed the name Sikkim is believed to be derived from 'Su' and 'Heem' which in the Limbu language means 'New House'. It is said that Tensong Namgyal a 17th century king had three wives. One was a Bhutanese, the second a Tibetan and the youngest a Limbu. He constructed a beautiful house for his Limbu queen at a place between Geizing and Pemayangtse monastery. He called it Suheem which eventually became Sikkim.

Although the name of the state is linked to a queen rom their community, the Limbus today suffer from a identity crisis." We are being clubbed as Nepalis. We are being clubbed as Hindus or Buddhists. The fact is we are a different people and we have our own separate religion. We are Limbus and we are animists. We worship nature, the various powers and manifestations of nature. It is called Yumaism. Our temple has no idols. We do not believe in idol-worship", a Limbu gentleman told me.

According to Yumaism there are 18 worlds in the universe ———— nine above the earth and nine below. The topmost world is the heaven and the lowest is the hell. The Limbus believe that the universe, plants and every living and non-living object, including human beings, were created by the infinite and eternal goddess, *Tagera Ninwaphuma*, whom they worship as their supreme deity. They are a deeply religious people and have a strong faith in their priests who perform all their rituals and ceremonies from birth to death. They have their own language and script called *Sirijunga,* named after the first Limbu king who unified *Dus-Limbuwan* ( ten Limbu fiefdoms spread over Sikkim and the district of Darjeeling). He also founded the Limbu script which is recognised as a state language and is taught in the schools of the state.

# Two Lakes, One Story

It is due to this age-old tradition of nature-worship that Sikkim is considered to be a holy land. Everything of Sikkim is sacred, its hills and lakes, rivers and jhoras, trees and woods. Earlier fishing in the lakes was considered an offence. Now cutting of trees could lead to imprisonment and even today people believe that those who are into timber-business never have a happy life.

This adoration for nature is a special aspect of Sikkim and nowhere is this better realized than at Khechodpalri lake where nature is such that one's mind is filled with veneration, where one's head bows in complete submission. It is a place of mystifying silence, as if Time has stopped, and that nothing exists beyond its periphery. The narrow trail that leads to it is a thick bed of fallen leaves which muffles one's footsteps. The lake itself is a huge expanse of clear water, so clear that it is said that if a leaf falls into it a bird appears from nowhere and takes it away.

At another end of Sikkim, in the extreme north there is another lake equally beautiful, if not more, but immensely formidable. Khechodpalri and Gurudongmar represent two extreme opposites, the contrast between the two is complete. At Khechodpalri nature seeps into you, it is within; at Gurudongmar nature overpowers, it is beyond. The former nestles in thick woods, amidst shay-shaying trees; at the latter there is not a blade of grass. The former is soothed by a cool, pleasant breeze; the latter is swept by haunting, howling wind. At Khechodpalri you submit yourself; at Gurudongmar you are insignificant, a non-entity in the magnificent amphitheatre of nature. The former is a Buddhist religious place, pure and simple. The latter is controversial; other faiths have laid claim to the shrine contending that it was Guru Nanak and not Guru Padmasambhava who had meditated by the lake. Incidentally, the former is the founder of the Sikh Panth while the latter is the venerable saint who converted Tibet to Buddhism. There are few who say that both are the same person. It caused considerable heartburn among the local people. But then the truly religious do not quarrel over places of worship; at least the Sikkimese do not. Thus while the lake has come to be known as Gurudongmar, a few still prefer to call it as Guru Nanak's lake. Khechodpalri is easily accessible: from Pelling it is Darrap, Rimbi falls, a few hamlets and you are there. Gurudongmar is assessible by jeep though considering the restrictions and the unpredictability of nature. To visit the place one has to acquire special permission from Gangtok as it is a high-security zone. And then after all the hassles, one's plans can go haywire if nature turns against you.

Having got a nod from important political circles we didn't have to run helter skelter for permission, neither did we have to worry about a vehicle. And nature too happened to be kind to us. One sunny morning we started out in two commander jeeps from Lachen. In the early hours Uttam had called us out to have a look at the mountains which were milky white, rising majestically above the green and rusted patches of the hills. Unfortunately I was feeling feverish. I had slept late having watched a fascinating dance performance at the lodge. But surely I was not going to let go of this opportunity!

We decided to make the journey step by step. First to Thangu from where depending on the weather we would decide. We travelled in the accompaniment of the Teesta and the scenario was rockier than what it is from Siliguri to Gangtok. We passed Yeong, a small habitation and there were clumps of rhododendrons here and there. It became chillier and I felt shivery. If this were the season, the entire stretch would have basked in blossoms, we were told. Someone spotted snow and our vehicle stopped. We hurled snow at each other like school children.

After about one hour's drive we reached Thangu. It is at 13500 ft and there was snow all around. We stopped by an army camp and after some chit-chat with the jawans, a Major greeted us. Kiran got busy clearing our passage to Gurudongmar. We were famished ——— —— none of us had had our breakfast. Major welcomed us in the army canteen ——— Dosa Point, where over a raging hearth crisp, fiery dosas were churned out along with lip-burning tea. As everyone concentrated on the food or on the seductive poster hung on the wall, I had a look around. In 1998 Thangu had a devastating avalanche. Twenty army men perished in their sleep. They never knew what hit them. Just opposite to the canteen there is a martyr's column commemorating their death. There are still signs of the disaster all around ———— damaged houses, piles of rubble accumulated at the foothills. Quarters have come up again in the landslide area itself, an indication of the perilous circumstances in which the army work. Some of us had a number of dosas and mugs of tea. When we left the Major warned us not to stay there beyond two o'clock. " You never know when the weather will change."

Beyond Thangu there is practically no habitation, except for the yak-herders. From here a narrow trail, a tough trek of several hours leads one to Muguthang where every year in the month of July yak races are held. An elderly gentleman of Mangan told me wistfully that in his childhood it was through Muguthang that his family used to go to Tibet, where his grandmother lived in a village in Shigatse. It used to be a trip on mules lasting several days. They would survive on their staple diet *tsampa,* powdered rice, and spend uncertain nights in the hostile terrain with only their patangs to defend themselves against roving pirates. There used to be lively, day-to-day contact in those days between the people of this region and those of Tibet. It was common to have relations on the 'other side' and as a people they were more close to the Tibetans than those down in the south.

We reached Yongdi from where our car rapidly made heights and the weather became very cold though the sun shone brilliantly. The rocky surrounds grew more snowy, the wind more gusty, the hills filled with snow-hangings, the trees suddenly turned into eerie white skeletons. Someone hummed, " *soldier, soldier, mithi baaten bol kor*" , someone plucked a handful of snow and Hindi-cinema like threw it all around. Our car danced over a thick slush of mud , the river occasionally vanished into thick sheets of ice.

We reached Goangong at a height of 17000 ft. Friendly, courteous jawans, spartan cottages, pictures of gods and goddesses, nude calendars, letters from home lying on a table and a crackling telephone. We had another round of hot tea which is really a godsend at such places. Our names and addresses were taken down and contact made with a forward post to clear our passage. Two jawans hopped into the back of our vehicle and one of them carried a jerry-can. The water of Gurudongmar is considered sacred; it can even make barren woman fertile.

From Goangong Teesta vanishes, its bed turns into a glacier. The frozen river runs parallel to the road and then suddenly, as if by magic, the landscape changes dramatically. So emphatic is the change that it makes everyone sit up, so stunning that it makes everyone gape in wonder. The river is lost, the hills are left behind; there are no woods, no trees, not even shrubs, no sign of any vegetation whatsoever. One is thrust into an immense, infinite expanse of snow, an awesome nothingness; where one sees only miles and miles of whiteness, where nothing stands in between one's eyes and the horizon, a breathtaking tableland of brutal beauty. If we had been in the ancient days one would have thought that this is the end of the earth, that there at the horizon is the apocalypse from where one would slip into an unending abyss of darkness.

No one talked. There were not even the oohs-oohs and aahs-aahs that one associate with seeing a beautiful place. Everyone was wonder-struck, overwhelmed by the sheer magnitude of the scenario, the sheer insignificance of human existence in the presence of almighty nature. We were moving through a military zone: bunkers, nozzles of guns peeping through the snow, billboards warning of mines, an abandoned helipad. There is no road here. Our vehicle zigzagged through the snow, the jawans guiding the driver. Since Yongdi the latter had been uneasy, complaining of dizziness. But he struck to his task. After about twenty minutes' drive we sighted a simple temple at the far end of the horizon beyond which were snow-clad mountains, Rajapahar and Ranipahar. Finally after negotiating a formidable hump our vehicle halted on a patch of leveled land, almost a courtyard, by the temple. By now everyone was feeling dizzy and staggered out of the car. There were jawans at the temple who informed over the telephone about our arrival. From the other side they queried about our health and asked if it was necessary to send a doctor.

The temple is a *sarvo-dharma-kendra*, an all religion centre. Inside on the altar is an idol of Buddha and another of Guru Nanak. We were treated to another round of tea. The sun shone and the entire landscape glistened and I felt warm. The lake was frozen. Nonetheless one of the jawans went down the slope into the lake and collected water. Others too filled up bottles to take back home. There are wild asses, *kaeung*, blue sheep in the area. Travel-operators in Gangtok and Calcutta churn out stories about the existence of snow-leopards. The more enthusiastic relate how in their childhood they used to wander into remote caves in the vicinity of the lake and discover with awe tell-tale footmarks of the elusive feline. A contractor of Lachen described to me how nearly three decades ago he with his men and mules used to walk the entire distance to Gurudongmar to supply provisions to the army. He has seen mules slip into the ravines below. He has often spent nights under the open sky or taken shelter in yak-herders' huts. The latter live in the plateau, their huts fortified by walls of thick slabs. Yak-herders from the other side of the border, from Tibet often slip into Indian soil. Where borders blur and boundaries are non-existent, such incursions are mostly routine. Sometimes though the Chinese are said to push in these simple folk to gather information about the Indian army's movements.

All of us stood in front of the lake and posed for a photograph. But then everyone talked of dizziness and were in a hurry to pack off; moreover we were nearing that two o'clock deadline set by the Major. The weather starts deteriorating from around this time. The scenario becomes fearsome; wind turns into a blizzard and the atmosphere is unreal. And on a bright moonlit night myriad, surreal images dance on the sparkling terrain.

# Djongu.com

Travelling in north Sikkim is always a delight. There is less rain, the sky is azure blue and the sun glorious. The woods are more dense, more green. There are many prayer flags along the roads, many stupas and chortens, more tell-tale signs that this is a predominantly Buddhist and BL territory. Gurudongmar was the climax of our trip to this region. But we also made other fascinating forays into places like Dzongu, Lachen and Lachung. One sunny morning in March, accompanied by Uttam and Norzeng, we were travelling to Dzongu, the home of the Lepchas, nestling deep into north Sikkim.

Uttam himself is a Lepcha but though his family still retains the surname, it has long shaken off the disadvantages of being born in a backward tribe. His father was once a chief engineer of the state. He married a Nepali and so has Uttam.

" In our family we celebrate all festivals —— Hindu, Buddhist or Christian", Uttam smiled as he flaunted the lockets around his neck, one of which was of Sai Baba, another a cross and a third reading ' Om Mani Padme Hum', the ubiquitous Buddhist mantra, meaning ' Hail, The Jewel In The Crown'. Lepchas were originally animists, many of whom later became Buddhists and Christians. Uttam's clan by marrying Nepali women has incorporated the Hindu faith as well, thus becoming a truly Sikkimese family.

Many of the kazis of Sikkim were of mixed Bhutia-Lepcha origin. Yabla, whose father was one of the most respected kazis of Sikkim, is a Lepcha and is proud to proclaim himself as one. There are however others who by virtue of their wealth and power have risen to a superior status and are at pains to hide their Lepcha origin.

We crossed the Rate Chu bridge, the gateway to north Sikkim where at a stream the Chogyal used to come fishing and where nearby his eldest son died in a car crash. This is the most volatile region of the state and the people here are fiercely proud and very temperamental. Candidates wanting to contest election from this district must acquire a macho image as people here like their representatives to be strong. They must also have enormous money power, to buy jackets and tracksuits for the youth, to make donations to clubs and associations and to arrange for food and drinks during festivals. Candidates end up spending huge sums long before the actual campaign begins. The scenario is similar to what it is in Arunachal Pradesh. There, during an election meeting the focus is on the drinks and the meat of *mithun*, a local cow that is freely distributed. Nobody is interested in what the leaders say.

We stopped at one Palden's place at Kabitingdam to have breakfast. We sat at a wooden house by the road. On its walls hung photographs of the chief minister Chamling and well, Jonty Rhodes.

" Are people interested in cricket here"? I asked.

" Just wait for sometime and you will find boys playing bat-ball on the road."

With regards to sports too Sikkim has integrated with the mainstream. Archery the original pastime has almost vanished. Soccer is still popular but cricket is fast catching up. *Khabser*, made of flour and *khapze chyadung*, made of maize, curly decorated snacks were offered to us to go with mugs of steaming tea. Palden is the local panchayat president and also secretary of the Green Valley club. Palden is a bold and fearless social worker. It is said that he once single-handedly stopped an eminent leader from entering north Sikkim. He had unsheathed his patang and obstructed his entry. Like many other young men of Sikkim he too has noble ideas about how to develop the state.

" Out of a total population of 6000 in this area

nearly 4500 live below the poverty line. There are not many jobs, even elaichi production has declined. We must start self-employment schemes for the poor like poultry, food-processing units etc."

Talented young go-getters men like Palden are frustrated with all the corruption, non-governance, the stark poverty that just refuses to go away.

" Something should be done before it is too late. We don't want to have terrorists here like in Jammu and Kashmir", the concern in Palden"s voice was genuine.

From Kabi we moved on and crossed Ramthan, Tanak, Namala, and then we left the main road to Mangan and took a different track that led to the land of the ' ravine folk'.

The Lepchas are called thus as they used to live isolated, in caves and atop trees. It is said that even now in the interiors they shy away at the sight of outsiders. The Lepchas also call themselves as Rongkups. The community has a rich oral tradition and folklore and they pride themselves as one of the few ancient races who have inherited the intriguing mythology of the Great Deluge, the others being the Aryans as described in the *Manu Smriti* and the Jews in the Deluge. It is here that I came to know about another version of the Teesta – Rangit story. It relates to a period when the Himalayas was just forming and the two rivers were yet to begin their respective journeys downwards from their sources, Naho and Nathor lakes as described in Lepcha folklore. It is said that an earthquake devastated the lakes and the rivers guided by *Parilbu* (King Serpent) and *Tutfo* ( Partridge ) guided them up to their confluence at Pazok, which is now called Peshok, and flooded the entire *Mayel Lyang*, the then Sikkim. The Lepchas who had gathered near mount Tendong, climbed atop the peak and prayed to the almighty to save them from the flood. Another earthquake occurred creating several high mountains around the northern zone of Mayel Lyang which resulted in the water flowing southwards thus saving the Lepchas from the Great Deluge. This mythology forms the basis of one of the most ancient festivals of the Lepchas which is observed in the month of August every year. It is called the *Tendong Hlo Rum Faat*, the worship of Mt. Tendong.

As we moved into the region the foliage became thicker. More cardamom, more waterfalls and more silence, interspersed with the cooing of strange birds and the rustle of a cool breeze. Soon the asphalt ceased and the road became dusty, narrower and at places quite inaccessible, emphasizing the fact that this is a more a neglected and underdeveloped area.

Decades earlier Chogyal Tashi Namgyal had turned Djongu into a restricted area to protect the Lepchas from outside influence, to ensure that they could live in peace and preserve their age-old culture and traditions.It is worth pondering as to how much of the idea has really worked. Lepchas constitute nearly two-thirds of the population while the rest live here on permits. Ironically it is the latter who control all the business and agricultural work while the Lepchas continue to languish in primitive condition. The situation could have been worse if a mega - hydroelectric project which had been announced in the area had been persisted with. It would have brought hordes of outsiders to the region and defeated the very purpose of making it a reserved area. It is said the Lepchas responded to this project by rolling down boulders on the first batch of workers. Being a prohibited zone, tourists are banned from entering the area. However with its rustic beauty Djongu could be turned into an ideal getaway for nature tourism. Tourists could be charged a fee which could be spend towards the area's development.

Tshering Lepcha joined us at Salimpakkel, the actual entry point to Djongu. He is a local. He studied in a local school and made a career elsewhere. But then he came back to take charge of his estate. He now has a business at Mangan and does social work in the area. On introduction he reeled off a list of names of villages which constitute Djongu —— Shipgyar, Sakyong Pentong, Tingum, Hegethong etc.etc. With him by my side we continued our journey till we came to stop by an elongated tribal hut. Beyond was the forest with a pedestrian trail trickling through it.

" I am afraid from here we have to make it on foot," smiled Tshering. Undaunted, we followed him. It wasn't much of a walk, barely of 15 minutes through thick woods perforated by arrows of sunrays. We were taken to two schools at Lick and Lingdam both of which were in appalling state. Broken windows, roofs caving in, blackboards propped up on bricks and students just passing time with no teachers in sight. Our visit was a welcome distraction though many of them were awe-struck with the intrusion of so many visitors.

How depressingly similar the state of education is all over the country be that in Sikkim, Bihar or West Bengal. It is for nothing that one- third of world's illiterate children belong to India. Schools are in appalling condition not only in Djongu, but anywhere from Gaya to Gajol or Jehanabad to Jangipur.

" Only there was some development during the Kazi"s time," moaned Tshering. He was of course referring to the first chief minister of the state.

" Roads were built, electricity also came to some areas but barely little has been done since then."

We returned to the Lepcha hut which is a combination of two chambers. It is quite a marvel since it is earthquake and landslide-proof. Outside the hut in the corner of a courtyard was a hearth with a raging fire. A charcoal-black kadai was on top of it with a whitish liquid furiously boiling and bursting bubbles.

" That's *roxy*, the local brew. Want to taste?" Norzeng smiled.

Suvendu discovered a rare opportunity of photographing a Lepcha family. They were all out in the courtyard. We settled down on stools and relished the brew, fresh from the fire as it were.

The family is engaged in wood-cutting and fruit-gathering. The young work in the cardamom fields or at construction. Selling roxy is also a source of income.

" You are not drinking?"

" I have stopped," Tshering said shyly.

" Actually after drinking people here get into lots of quarrels and brawls. I have to take care of all that."

" Huh," Norzeng burst out laughing, the same kind of roar that accompanied us on the journey, the laughter that ricochets off the hills. He is a real livewire, a genius at leg-pulling.

" So you are now Tshering Guha and he is Somnath Lepcha."

" Suvendu are you drinking?"

Sensing what he was trying to get at, Suvendu nodded and said, " a sip or two."

" So you are now Suvendu Lepcha and he is Tshering Chatterjee."

The entire gathering burst out laughing.

The session went on for long. Bottles vanished as quickly as they were filled in. " Nowhere will you get it as fresh," Tshering encouraged us. In between, our appetite was whetted by plates of noodles. When we finally took leave shadows had lengthened and the sun had drifted to the western horizon.

On our way back I almost committed a harakiri. We stopped by a bridge and, well, what a bridge that was! It was a pontoon in the most devastating state of neglect. It was across a river 30m in breadth, most of which were rocks rather than water. It hung tantalizingly supported by cables severely worn with use and from which torn fibers looped into the riverbed below. Its platform was in a worse state with deadly gaping holes and planks jutting out in mid air, the whole thing ready to collapse any moment.

" You can do it", everyone goaded me.

" Look even school children are crossing it".

" The other side is the more interior part of Djongu. This is the only link between the two sides. People use it everyday".

I was being taken for a ride; the tragedy is that I didn't realize it then. Before I knew it I was almost half way into the bridge, precariously dangling , hanging on to the ropes for dear life. I looked back only to find the blurred faces of my companions some distance away. There was concern on their faces, the leg-pulling had given away to a sudden grimness, the discovery of which made my legs wobbly. I looked below and thought the rocks were stretching upwards to gobble me up, as if the trickling stream had suddenly developed into a gigantic whirlpool.

" Don't look down", Tshering barked as he held me up by my armpits.

" Look straight ahead. Don't worry, I am here".

One tentative step after another, and another, another. Careful with every move lest I step into those gaping holes or on snapped fibers and broken planks. Not once did I look back again, not once did I look down. I looked straight as an arrow like a robot with Tshering pushing and prodding me on to the other end where I collapsed on a slab and announced, " I am not going back".

Tshering took some time to response.

" Now you know how precariously the people here live. You have experienced it yourself".

If I had a pistol I could have shot him. Instead I sat holding my head as the haze of roxy was beginning to clear off.

" There are no roads this side. You have to walk all the way to Mangan".

As an afterthought he added, " I could accompany you".

That bridge symbolises the utter absurdity of the times we live in. At a time when technological inventions abound, when human cloning is in the realm of the possible, when there is talk of even cracking the immortality code, life on the other side of that bridge is pre-historic: where a solitary trail is the only road, where human feet are the only mode of transport, where there is no electricity, no telephone, where people's dwellings are startlingly similar to what cavemen used millenniums ago. What similarity does a Lepcha in Djongu have with a computer professional in the Silicon valley except that they are biologically similar. While the latter represent the pinnacle of development in science and technology, the former is not even aware of inventions made centuries ago. Even in the new millennium the Lepchas of Djongu does not have access to the barest essentials. He still only has a cloth around his waist, survives on meagre forest produce, and lives in his own ghetto cut off from the rest of the world. Inspite of both being homo sapiens the difference between them is so enormous that they could be construed as two separate species altogether.

# The Twin Valley

We halted for the night at Mangan and there at the hotel we met Sonam Dorjee. Tall and handsome, he has a good educational background. He has worked in high-profile capacities in various parts of the country. Later he returned to Sikkim and tried out his luck in politics. Indeed he became the 'Officer on Special Duty' to the chief minister Pawan kumar Chamling. Thereafter he resigned and was waiting for the right offer to come along from rival political parties. By virtue of his education in Darjeeling he knew a spattering of Bengali and could even sing a song or two. Sonam belongs to a very respectable family of Mangan and when I told him that I had been to Djongu, he told me the story of the Tholung monastery.

The monastery is in Djongu, a 25 kms walk from a place called Linzey. It was built in the eighteenth century by the Chogyal, Chakdor Namgyal. It is one of the most secluded gompas of Sikkim hidden by thick forests and high forbidding cliffs. It is in this monastery that the monks kept their most valuable scriptures, artifacts and other relics to save these from the invading armies which periodically trampled the little kingdom. The monastery is also said to possess chortens containing the ashes of respected rimpoches. The ancestors of Sonam were in charge of the monastery from its very inception. His family members looked after the upkeep of the estate while there were others who contributed towards the expenses. He told us that the original structure was demolished about a decade ago and a new one came up in 1991. The monastery also runs a school at Linzey. Even now Sonam's elder brother, who lives at Mangan looks after the estate. It is said that in the earlier days armed monks used to guard the revered gompa day and night lest any invading foreigner sneak into its premises. Times have changed. The only sounds now heard at the Tholung monastery are the pat-pat of the prayer flags and the humming of mantras by the handful of monks.

Next morning we headed for Chungthang, on the way to Lachen and Lachung. Like the Gurudongmar lake there is also a shrine at Chungthang which is shared by the Sikh and the Buddhist communities. Here there is a monastery and a gurudwara side by side. There is a rock the imprint on which is said to be the footmark of Guru Padmasambhava. There is a hole into the rock which is filled with holy water. It is said that the revered Guru, had a meal sitting on the rock after which he had sprinkled the leftover in the surrounding area. It is in this adjacent area that paddy grows defying the rocky conditions and the height of the town which is close to 6000 ft. The Sikhs on the other hand maintain that it was Guru Nanak instead who had meditated on the rock.

Chungthang is a lovely place lying at the confluence of the Lachen chu and Lachung chu, two little titillating streams which lead to the twin valley of Lachen and Lachung. The people of these two picturesque villages are called Lachenpas and Lachungpas respectively. They belong to the mongoloid race and are fiercely proud of their heritage and like their valiant ancestors have martial characteristics. It is said that in the earlier days the south of the Donkiala pass was the territory of the Lachungpas and the north that of the Lachenpas. It is also said there was once a raging dispute over who controlled the Cholamoo lake, the origin of the river Teesta. Again a little ahead of Chungthang at a place called Denga a waterfalls demarcates the areas of the Lepchas and the Lachenpas. Skirmishes over hegemony of land was a routine affair in those days which ultimately was settled by an exchange of cash and yak meat.

We went to Lachung on a wrong day : elections were near and various political parties were holding meetings by the river side. The river here is strong and vibrant. Stages had been set up on the barren ground adjacent to it from where political leaders of various hues were rendering their sermons. We sighted Sonam who was going around with a hat on and looked like a character straight out of a cowboy movie. Finding no interest in the speeches, we wandered through the town. It was strangely quite and ghostly with almost all the shops closed and repair works going on at a reputed resort. Finally we entered a café and asked the lady who was busy at the kitchen where everyone had gone. She said that while many had gone to the meetings, the others had closed shop for fear of trouble. It is symptomatic of how deeply political the Sikkimese society is. Later there was an incident where even a religious festival, the traditional *cham* (ceremonial lama dances) observed at the Lachen monastery was on the verge of being cancelled as the monks themselves were divided into rival political camps and each wanted to perform the age-old ritual on their own. It was only at the intervention of the chief minister himself that the cham was held on the due date with all the traditional pomp and grandeur.

Suvendu had been to Lachung once before. It was in the days when he was still under the hangover of communism and believed that to know a people one has to live and eat as they do. So he stayed with a poor family, drank chhang and ate yak meat. He never went to sleep that night. For the first few hours he hovered between the loo and his room trying to tame a raging diarrhoea and later sensing that something was seriously wrong he woke up his driver and asked him to take him to Gangtok. "Fast", he barked. The hapless driver, one Thomas, who had several times warned him against taking yak meat, worked up a furious speed and dumped him into the Gangtok hospital in the wee hours of the morning. The doctors gave Suvendu a dressing down saying that even the local people thought several times before taking the dreaded meat thus ending his adventure on a sorry note.

Yak though is very much an utility animal in Sikkim as much as the cow is in the gangetic plains. However it can survive only at a height above 10000 ft. and the ones that are found in the lower ranges are dzos a cross-breed of yak and cow. People, particularly the poorer sections, eat yak meat. Its hide and hair are used for making wrappers, bags and coarse garments. Its milk is used towards making churpi. It is a sturdy, reliable carrier of goods and as benign and domestic as the cow. It is also used for entertainment, like at the Chhangoo lake, where the animal takes children on jolly rides. Unlike the cow though the Yak has no holy connotations, though that in no way detracts from its usefulness or the affection the people have for this docile animal.

The café where we were sitting was clean. The utensils were sparkling and the lady was rustling up

something in the oven. Rolls of yak meat were hung on the wall and a sinister black cat sat in the corner.
I felt uneasy. " Why don't you drive that cat away, at least as long we are here?"

The lady gave me a cold look and said : " It brings good luck. As long as it has been in this house, we have prospered."

" Which party you belong to", she asked a little later.

" Neither", I said. " We are from Calcutta."

" Oh, many tourists come from there. Have some pork." She served us two plates of pork. Suvendu flinched and would have none of it and even after the lady repeatedly reassured that it was not yak meat, he remained struck to his drinks.

The woods around Lachung is thick and rich with various medicinal plants and herbs. Until recently the people were ignorant about the importance of these plants and outsiders used to smuggle them out with ease. It is said that a very valuable plant called *ercha gumbuk* is available in abundance here. A Lachungpa told me that the same plant is available in Tibet as well and was used by the Chinese to enhance the performances of their athletes. Apple-farming is a major agricultural activity at Lachung and now there is renewed emphasis on tea which used to be grown in abundance in the days of barter trade with Tibet. Lachen on the contrary is more rocky but recently joint forest management programmes have been launched at both these places to protect the environment.

One of the oldest forms of democracy exist at both Lachen and Lachung. People of both these places practice the *Pipon* system, a time-tested form of grass-root democracy. It is a modified Tibetan system and is actually a derivative of *Chipon*———— Chi meaning accounts and Pon meaning person who keeps the accounts. The Pipon decides on the allocation of jobs in the local area, supervises the construction of roads and developmental activities. Bidding for various works is done in hard cash. The bidders names are written on wooden blocks and put into a bag. A lama puts his hand into the bag and brings out a block and the person whose name is written on it gets the job. There is an annual membership fee to the Pipon and the persons who gets a job or work also pay donations. This is the Pipon's source of revenue, the profit from which is distributed amongst the members at the end of the year. A portion of the profit is also donated to the local monastery.

We halted for the night at the Lachen bungalow. There in its spartan confines we had a very spartan meal. A little later someone told us that a lot of fun was going on at the Gurudongmar lodge which was just opposite to the place from where we were staying. We ventured into the lodge and found ourselves in the midst of a carnival. Men and women formed a circle holding each others hands, singing and dancing and maintaining the rhythm with supple and intricate feet movements. Around them on low chokseys sat the motley crowd, clapping, cheering and drinking. Everyone was there : Uttam, Norzeng and Sonam, still with his hat on. We joined in and tried to match the rhythm but soon fell out unable to match the heady beat. Whenever anyone fell out in similar fashion there were jeers and the ladies in particular broke out in shrill laughter. It was not only us who failed but there were many locals as well who could not handle the rhythm. Indeed it was too wild for us outsiders to comprehend. Norzeng was ecstatic and shouted that finally he was with his own people. I was hypnotised by the seductive monotony of the rhythm, the heady beat of the music in the background and the shrewd elegance with which the ladies kept the men at bay and I never knew when I went to sleep.

# Freedom at Kewzing

'Guru' is Guru Rimpoche, 'Dong' is face and 'Mar' is red: Gurudongmar means red-faced Guru Rimpoche, Yabla explained to us at his farmhouse at Kewzing. Incidentally according to most people Guru Rimpoche and Guru Padmashamvabha are the same but for a few the latter is one of the eight manifestations of the former. We had taken an early morning trekker to that place which however did not go beyond Ravang as there were not enough passengers. From here Kewzing is 6 kms for which we had to take another vehicle. Ravang has indeed changed a lot. The market area was busthing with people and the road busy with cars and trekkers. I looked up at the SBI office. Alas! Duttada was no longer there. Hotel Mainam has been taken over by its original owner. Kishoreda has started a new hotel. Ravang now has five hotels and a resort as well. Kewzing is almost like what Ravang was four years ago. Sleepy, with few people, boys playing cards, shops without buyers, market without a buzz. There is no hotel. There is a bungalow which can be booked from Gangtok. It is mentioned in David-Neal's book. It is at this bungalow that the author and Sidekong Tulku, the tenth Chogyal had a miraculous encounter with a famous seer of those times.

Everyone knows Yabla. His house is 15 minutes walk from here but there was no vehicle to give us a lift. The walk is easy, we were told. But we worried about the luggage and there were no coolies either. Two boys accompanied us up to a distance after which we continued down a muddy path, a divergence from the main road. We need not have worried about a vehicle for we walked downhill and even with the luggage it was cool. We emerged from the woods and on to a ground at the edge of which stood an old-fashioned but stately house.

" Yabla", Suvendu asked two men slumbering in the sun. We followed their direction and were facing another house less ethnic but equally stately with a cute little cottage by its side.

" Welcome, welcome", Yabla called out standing on the terrace which was like a hanging verandah extended out of the upper floor of the house.

" I am the king here. This is my kingdom", he laughed aloud.

Well, he truly is. It is a sprawling estate of 40 acres covering hills and valleys, woods and plains. The house we first saw is his ancestral house which he has turned into a prayer hall and a rest-house for monks. Its adjacent part is more ancient and has a kitchen, a store and a dining space. There is an outhouse, servant's quarters where 4-5 families live. In front of it is a tilled land where potatoes, ginger and other vegetables are grown. There is a solar cell adjacent to it the electricity from which is used towards agriculture. There is also a piggery and a tin-roofed garage by the older house. And there are a few chortens and the open space between the two houses circled with prayer flags mounted on strong and erect poles. They fluttered merrily in the strong breeze, making sweet music to the ear. At the back of the house it is the wilds amidst which atop another hill nestles the Tashiding monastery. The woods continue into the hills beyond which as if popping up from nowhere are the gleaming peaks of Karbu, Narsing, Simvo, Kanchenjungha lined up as if in a firing squad, or a parade of delectable ice-creams. Suvendu meanwhile was downstairs and was taking photographs here, there and everywhere. The mountain range, the house, the chortens, prayer flags, he was shooting all over the place.

" This is a domestic area, Suvendu. You have to pay for those pictures", Yabla again roared with laughter.

" It must be very lonely here."

" Not at all. I have my people around. I play with their children." Then he abruptly stood up and pointed his arm pistol-like towards a child playing on the ground.

The latter froze, his palms locked in namaste.

" Click, Suvendu."

Moments passed.

" It's like playing statue", Suvendu said.

Yabla relaxed and the child went back to playing, swinging around a flag-pole and singing, " *dil to pagal hai,dil diwana hai.*"

Bollywood has reached where the state has not. The lure of Hindi songs is universal.

Yabla of course is quite a fan of Bollywood. He would often be humming old numbers like *yeh saam masatani.*" In Bombay he relished his roles of glorified extras, being beaten up by the hero, and sleeping with whores. Having made the cardinal sin of being related to the Chogyal, every week he had to report to the local than a lest he escapes to some foreign country.

" Even my children do not want to stay here. Somehow they will spend the morning and then become restless wanting to leave as soon as possible. They prefer living in Gangtok. I wanted to present that cottage to my wife on her birthday. Come let's have a look."

The cottage is compact and exudes refined taste. In the basement there is a sit-out, a cellar and a fire-place. Above is a bedroom with a collection of books. There are Grishams, Sheldons, Wallaces and even Rushdie's latest ' Ground Beneath Her Feet'. There are books on

Sikkim, Life and National Geographic and a host of coffee-tablers.

" We could spend days here just going through these books", I exclaimed. Suvendu began to browse through 'Tibet in Exile', I involved myself with a gazette on Sikkim.

" Look all this I wanted to present to her. But she would have none of it. Then I tried other ways. I said I am a common man not a saint. Don't encourage my infidelity by leaving me alone in this lonely place."

So did she finally concede?

" No", Yabla sighed. " She said whatever you do I am not going to that lonely place."

He kept the cottage to himself, a huge test of his fidelity. Earlier the estate was much bigger. Since his father's death it has been divided between Yabla and his two brothers. His father was a Kazi holding a first class magistrate's power. He looked after law and order in the area, solved disputes and gave out judgement. He could mete out six months' of imprisonment and fine up to RS 5000.

" Everyone asks me to use the title Kazi. But why should I? I am not a Kazi, my father was."

" But weren't the Kazis very ruthless people?"

" My father reduced the house tax ————*-dhuri*

*khazana*. He also did not allow bonded labour in his estate. Others also were beginning to see the writing on the wall."

We went down for lunch. A leftover sun caressed the hills, the woods the tip of the house and the flags still fluttered merrily.

" Let's take left."

We circled the ground from the left. It is sacred, the flags indicate that. But why left?

" It's just intuition. We also take the right but never across."

The ancestral house is nearly hundred years old. The kitchen part is linked to it with a small wooden bridge. The kitchen is surprisingly traditional almost like the one we saw at the Lepcha house at Djongu. There is an open hearth above which is a rack stacked with logs. Beside this there are utensils, mostly brass and wooden. Below at the corner is the sink. Opposite to it is the storeroom with dry meat hanging from the ceiling.

We had lunch in large brass thalis, the kind our grandmothers used and which till recently used to be an important item in a trousseau when she leaves for her in-laws house.

Yabla had arranged a meeting with Captain Yongda. Since we had arrived he had been trying desperately to contact Captain over his cellphone. Finally when he did make contact he found that Captain was away to a for wedding. However he left word that we would reach the monastery by the evening. After lunch we left in Yabla's car. We refurbished our stock of cigarettes at Legship. The shopkeeper was from Mainaguri in north Bengal. He had come to Legship way back in 1978. I had also found a Bengali tailor at Kewzing. Who says the Bengalis are not enterprising!

The sky was clear with stars shining, quite unusual in this part of Sikkim. There were stars on the hills as well, domestic lights, yellowish and blinking in the darkness. And then there was an intricate constellation of lights: Rangitnagar. It refused to leave us. With every turn in the hills that constellation would zoom up from nowhere, as if we were orbiting in space and Rangitnagar was another galaxy.

Suddenly the weather deteriorated rapidly. It rained heavily and the wind was strong and unpredictable. The temperature too dipped and I rolled down the windows. Visibility became poor and our driver made slow progress. I looked up to the sky and found that a thick veil of cloud had covered the glittering canopy and to think that I was counting stars only a few minutes ago. It was past eight o'clock when we reached the monastery and the entire arena was deserted. The gompa looked like an imposing castle and the surrounding prayer flags fluttered wildly in the blustery wind. Our driver stepped out and called out several names. There was no response whatsoever and we asked him not to get wet. We were weighing the option of going up to Pelling and checking into hotel Garuda when suddenly three boys emerged from the shadows lighting up the courtyard with their torches. They were shivering in the cold and offered to help us with our luggage. However we picked up our bags and ran into the building. Our driver left : he had a long and risky journey ahead of him.

Captain had not yet arrived. There were no guests at the monastery. The school was closed. Students and the lama boys were on vacation. A few of them were there; they had returned early for extra classes.

"It's cold, isn't it?" I asked.

" Last year was better. It's too cold this time. We pray to Guru Padmasambhava not to make it too cold", a boy said shivering.

He showed us into our room. There were two cots, a hanger, a small table. The boy brought a jug of water. Fortunately there were enough blankets.Captain came sometime later by which time our dinner was served. He couldn't recognize us but nonetheless invited us to his prayer-room. Poor boys! They were preparing to go to sleep but now they too had to follow behind us. A single diya was burning on the altar. There were candles, tumblers, flasks, bottles of distilled water and an empty bottle of whisky. Captain drank from a small cup called *phukyo.* " What is the dress that you are wearing called?" He was in a monk's habit but it's gown was up to the knees and the sleeves of the upper were baggy and meticulously creased.

" It was given to me by a Malaysian Chinese monk. He said he had acquired it from the north of Afghanistan."

" How was the marriage?"

" It was O.K. This is the season and lots of marriages are taking place. Today itself I attended two."

" It would have been nice to attend a Sikkimese marriage."

" I could have taken you along if you came in the morning."

The boys sitting on cushions were struggling to keep awake. One was actually dozing off.

We talked about his school, monastery, rimpoches, Prince Wangchuk.

" Prince! But he is the Chogyal", Captain was offended. Many Sikkimese still refer to him as the Chogyal.

Wild stories go around him and the Palace. He has become a sadhu. He meditates in high caves, in Nepal and Bhutan. That there are no telephone connections to the Palace and that one would not be able to recognize him when he is moving around. A Calcutta businessman told me that around Diwali he comes to the city to perform a religious rite called *prandaan*, which means to give back life. He is accompanied by several senior monks and they buy huge quantities of fish which they release in the Ganges. Asked as to why they do not do it in Sikkim itself, the businessman said that the rivers there being much smaller there is no guarantee that the fish will survive.

" Whenever he comes to the monastery he asks about the monks, about their well being. Often I have to hide because I can not confess to him about the truth: that they are not well fed, or that they are not having the right education."

Captain was still struggling with his school. The Muyal Liang Trust of which he is the chairman planned to accommodate 225 children for the year 1999-2000. However due to lack of funds it could only accept 186. The school is badly in need of maintenance, additional classrooms, teaching equipments, teachers' quarters. The bakery and carpet weaving centres are also not functioning properly. The International Heritage Meditation Centre at the monastery which has been built to provide for studies of ancient Sikkimese practices of meditation and worship is in need of electrical and sanitary furnishings.

" You have seen the rooms. I cannot even provide my guests a room-heater."

Suvendu I and took turns to go out and have a smoke. It was late night and I felt sorry for the boys.

" I will be helpful to government of India", Captain said earnestly.

" They don't have to pay me. I will work for our culture. There are destitute children in my school. Let the government at least provide salary to the teachers. I will arrange food and lodging for my students."

While walking to Pelling the next day we had a look at the school. It is now a three-storied building. There is still no girls' hostel and presently they put up at Captain's home at Tikjuk. There is a playing ground and there are plans to start a rock-climbing course nearby. Occasionally Captain would pick up conversation with passing children. " Collect the cowdung in the ground and dump it in the tea gardens." The school has a tea-garden at Tikjuk as well.

At another point he stopped a group and asked them to sing the school song. Standing stiff they promptly broke out into a chorus:

We the children of DPC Academy
Here have gathered to wish you TASHI DELE

At Pelling Captain's family hotel Phamrong, which we had found under construction last time, was now complete. 'Pham' means dakini and 'rong' means falls. It is now the costliest hotel in Pelling catering mainly to foreign tourists. There are American and European suites and I jokingly asked Captain why he had forgotten about the Indians. In its lobby there is a map of the kingdom of Sikkim. Now there are 38 hotels in Pelling. Heavy tourist traffic is taking its toll on the area. During the last season there was an acute scarcity of water and one had to buy a bucket of water for Rs 10.

Our programme was to return to Kewzing along with Captain where Yabla said he would light the chimney at his cottage and we would have a discussion on every topic on earth. We had some time on our hands till his car came to pick us up. We wandered into hotel Garuda and once again had a little discussion with Wangdi. The place had changed. Most of the posters in the restaurant were gone and the TV, a coloured one, was now at the reception. Wangdi warmed himself by a room-heater. A black cat sat at his feet and a programme on Bosnia was going on in the TV. This is the last time I met Wangdi whose views on Sikkim I have always appreciated. I asked him if it is true that there is a change in China's attitude towards religion in Tibet. Some people told me that China is now renovating monasteries and sincerely caring for the monks.

" Not because they respect Buddhism. But because Tibet is a big tourist attraction. It brings them foreign exchange."

I also told him that some people harboured the fond idea that Sikkim would have been better off with China than with India.

" Only when you wear the shoe you know how it pinches. We have no idea how it is to live with China. Nobody who is emotional can live with China. Look they cannot even tolerate Falun Gong which is not even a full-fledged religion. It is only a sect which practice meditation. Think then what they have done to Buddhism in Tibet and what they would have done to Sikkim."

This is the big reason why the Sikkimese have accepted the merger gracefully. By and large India has not tampered with the religious and cultural traditions of Sikkimese people. There have been instances when Buddhist relics have been vandalised or chortens destroyed. But these have been mainly aberrations and most importantly not a calculated state assault rather the handiwork of local jealots. Unfortunately the same cannot be said of Tibet where from the very outset China has been bent upon destroying the edifice of Tibetan Buddhism with a vengeance.

Back at Yabla's house we were welcomed with chhang. We sat in the cottage around the fire-place with Yabla's boys occasionally feeding the fire with logs. Captain went back to his prison days, to his days in Baharampur jail when he was detained under the ' Maintenance of Internal Security Act' (MISA) during the emergency time. Along with him was Bhandari and two others and they were kept in a cell with petty thugs and criminals. The jail was then swarming with naxalites and other party activists. Captain used to hold prayers everyday and perform puja. A tall, handsome man who was the dada in the prison took a liking to Captain. " Arre, you are a sadhu, why have they kept you with the criminals?" he would say. He pulled strings and Captain and his group were shifted to a separate cell. Not only that, he fixed up other prisoners to fetch their water, food, clean up their room. He also saw to it that they received the best provisions. Thereafter Captain not only held his prayers more elaborately but also distributed prasad to everybody.

" What are your future plans Captain?" I asked.

" Let's see if funds are forthcoming. I will wait for another couple of years, may be and then consider the offers I have from other countries to set up a similar school there."

One of the offers is from Argentina and we met

one person from that country at the monastery. " I am the big brother of Diego Maradona", he had said on being introduced. Actually he is based in Venezuela where he is a radio-broadcaster. He is seeking Captain's help to put up a chorten in his home town. He was also asking him to hold a prayer for the thousands of people who had been marooned in floods in Venezuela. " It is the biggest disaster in the history of Latin America", he told us.

" I don't want to leave Sikkim. But what do I do? Even my family feels I am wasting my time. They don't support my social work. Only my elder daughter provides me emotional and financial support."

Next morning we raided Yabla's library. While browsing through a coffee-tabler named 'Monasteries in the Himalayas' we searched if there was anything on Sikkim. "You won't find it so easily", Captain winked. "Sikkim is a hidden land, you know." "Bayul Denzong?" I asked. He nodded smiling.

Bayul Denzong is the Promised Land of the Sikkimese, the land of milk and honey, wisdom and treasure. The Sikkimese believe that , as ordained by Guru Padmasambhava, someday they will have to set out for that hidden land. A handful feel that already that time has come what with the jhoras drying up, cardamom production falling and people hardpressed to retain their identities on their own soil.

Yabla has the habit of collecting paper-cuttings of important news items. One such was on the land rights of BLs. According to a Revenue Order issued in 1917 other communities are barred from acquiring the land of the BLs. Now various communities are demanding the repeal of this restriction. Since the BLs are now categorised as Scheduled Tribes, ironically these communities are also willing to be categorised as thus as that will enable them to lay claim to protected Bhutia-Lepcha land. Fortunately neither the state or the centre has so far showed any inclination to heed to their demand. On the other hand while some BLs resent being referred to as tribals, they can not deny the fact that the ST status gives them significant advantages.

During this visit there was an incident which I have not been able to dismiss as one of mere coincidence. At Yabla's house Captain asked Suvendu to photograph a black crow sitting on a tree.

" It has come with some message. It also comes to the monastery occasionally."

I dismissed it as humbug.

Later when we were having tea at Geizing and toying with the idea of staying the night there, Captain who had gone out to catch up with some acquaintances, suddenly came back and asked us to come with him to

Tikjuk as someone of his family was seriously ill. We rushed to his home, which is twenty minutes' drive from there, and found an old lady in coma. A local monk was conducting prayers and carrying out traditional healing.

Captain was understandably upset and reminded us about that crow: "Didn't I tell you that it has brought some message."

The lady was 73 years old. She was brought up by Captain's grandfather. One day in his village some Brahmins came to him and asked for his permission to stay on his land till cultivation began. There were some women in the group including one who was pregnant. His grandfather consented. One morning when he took his cattle to graze in the forest he heard a baby crying. He found her in the bushes and brought her home. Later he went to the Brahmins' busti and asked them if the baby was theirs. Initially they denied but later they broke down and said that a girl born on *amavasya*, new moon, brings bad luck to the family for which they had abandoned her in the forest. Captain's grandfather not only kept the baby but gave them a kilo of butter as well. Unfortunately the baby could not be provided with milk and was brought up on chhang fed with straw. Later in life it grew to be her obsession. She got married, had children who were later well settled but her addiction to the brew only strengthened with years. Captain had tried to settle her at the monastery and even promised her a daily ration of two kodos, pipes of chhang but in vain. It is a tribute to her vitality that seven decades of that heady brew had laid her low only at the ripe age of 73 and not much earlier.

# Another Election

As the elections neared, Uttam once again jumped into politics. When I called him up just a few months before the polls, he was excited: "Somnath, we are surely coming to power. Why don't you just come over and attend some of our meetings. You can judge for yourself."

I wasn't one to miss this opportunity and landed up at Uttam's house within a week. "He is very busy nowadays. Politics is a funny game isn't it", his father said. I was savouring a plate of sael rotis, which are made of rice, and coffee when Uttam barged in. He was tense and I instantly knew that the political scenario in the state was once again hotting up. I asked him the inevitable question which he always knew I was going to ask.

" Look for twenty years I have been in the opposition, it's my turn now. Bhandari is coming up like never before. This is my big chance. Most of my friends have joined SSP. He has given me a good post in the organisation."

I kept quiet. I hadn't even been surprised when he had told me about it over the phone. During all my years of knowing him I have become accustomed to his fickleness.

" Many SDF people have joined us. Sikkim Ekta Manch have merged with us. You cannot believe the support we are getting."

Even in Calcutta I had heard that Bhandari was coming up. But elections were still months away. SDF has the advantage of being in power, not to mention the fact that it had done reasonably well during its tenure, managed to keep the various sections of the people reasonably happy. Most importantly the 1994 election was a watershed in Sikkim's politics. It marked the rise of the OBCs, their consolidation into a powerful vote bank. Like in the Hindi heartland caste equations are no longer what they used to be in the 80s. At least for me, an outsider, a lay observer, the picture didn't look too good for SSP.

But Uttam kept repeating about being twenty years in the opposition and when he had run out of all arguments he delivered the coup-de-grace: " But the BBC has predicted that we will come to power."

Early next morning we left for Rakdong Tintek, a constituency in east Sikkim. This is a reserved seat for BLs and is an instance of how the parity system has been violated over the years. The definition of the BL category was diluted in 1978 to include other communities like

Sherpas, Tibetans, Chumbipas, Yolmos and at the same time the number of reserved seats was reduced from 15 to12. Thus the BLs have to be content with lesser number of seats though the category now includes many other communities. The Bhutia community in particular demanded an amendment to the Sikkim Scheduled Tribe Order (1978) which has categorised the above non-Bhutia ethnic groups as 'Bhutia'. In the 1999 elections also all the parties fielded Sherpa candidates from this constituency which resulted in a lot of resentment among the BLs. Some organisations boycotted the polls while others staged relay hunger strikes in the capital.

We stopped at a village called Kokalay. There were few scattered houses, one of which was decked up with flags and festoons. It was a small house at the edge of a cliff. In front of it a plastic sheet was spread on the slope. People sat on it, relaxed as if they were sitting on a gallery. The leaders were welcomed with khadas and garlands and ladies smeared their forehead with sindoor. There were around 50 people, excluding the cadres and the security personnel. I suddenly became a prominent person around. Someone had spread the news that I had come all the way from Delhi to cover the campaign. The speeches began. An old man brought out a garland from a carrybag and garlanded Bhandari. A small girl approached him with a thali on which he dropped a few hundred rupee notes, and then quite unlike any political leader I have seen, fished out a small camera and took her snap. For us habituated to meetings attended by thousands, massive demonstrations, claustrophobic crowds, this was an absolutely delightful experience. The interaction between the leader and the people was intimate, without any barriers as if it were a Sunday morning tete-a-tete. At the next meeting at Tunim Barang the procedure was similar ———————— khadas, garlands, sindoor, dropping of notes on a thali. Here the meeting was held on a small ground with a narrow path leading to it lined with banana stems. By this time everyone was hungry and I was led into a cottage where I was offered a bun to go with a thali of maggy soup, more soup than maggy, rather as Norzeng said, maggy *jhol.* Some rice was lying on an aluminium thali from which everyone grabbed a handful and mixed it with the jhol. When we were about to finish one of Uttam's friends, whose in-laws live in Calcutta, brought in a plate of eggs and called out, " *moshai, taratari.*" To cap it all Uttam wangled a bottle of roxi from somewhere and everyone forgot about the food.

Needless to say that carnival like atmosphere did not remain. As election neared, tension rose, clashes erupted. During my next visit I found Uttam more tense and at the same time more confidant about his party's victory. He was totally committed to the party and hardly had any time to spare for us. He had closed down his travel agency, sold out all his equipments ——————— — tents, sleeping bags and even the cameras.

" I need the money for the campaign", he told me.

" What if your party loses?"

" Firstly that's not going to happen. *Phir bhi* I can start all over again."

His wife had passed law and she was practising at the local court. The travel agency has now been turned into her chamber.

" She is doing very well. She handles our party cases also", Uttam said.

It was quite late. The hotel lobby had quietened down. There was little noise of traffic on the road.

" *Arre bhai,* twenty years is not a matter of joke. Just think of it : for twenty years I have been in the opposition. You just see now what happens." He was very hopeful about the future.

" I am not going to contest. I will be a party man and once we come to power we can start that magazine of ours. You will do the writing and I and Suvendu will do the photographs."

" What about R.C. Poudyal why did you leave him?" I suddenly asked.

" Oh! R.C. Either he is mad or he is a genius."

" I went to meet him after the last election. I sat wanting to talk to him and all the while he gestured to me to remain quiet. He was in *maunabrata*, silence. I was disgusted and after sitting for a long time I left."

I threw smoke rings in the air and occasionally looked at the TV which was sending silent pictures of a one day match.

" His son died. He was studying in Delhi, perhaps suicide. The whole town gathered during the funeral. I too went."

Next day while Uttam left for the west to solve some disputes, I went to meet R.C, to find out whether he is mad or a genius. I enquired about him in his Ranipool residence. Bhabhiji was there and she accompanied me for the rest of the way. She talked falteringly about the misfortune, her eyes brimming with tears. That house like the rebel of the 60s was now vagabondish. Long weeds covered the entrance, cowdung was littered everywhere, the garden hardly existed. R.C.Poudyal the man who made the merger possible, the man who triggered that fateful, decisive agitation against the Chogyal, sat in the sun, his face a jungle of hair, his eyes sparkling, his little frame crowded by a pile of books. He looked like a sadhu, like a brown Jesus.

Gradually he recognised me and when he finally recollected he said: " when you are an old friend and have come from as far as Calcutta, I owe it to you to spare you some time. As it is I don't meet anyone these days. I am observing *roja* and I am also into my studies."

" Roja", I exclaimed. I thought he was a devout Hindu.

" It is good to observe roja, fasting is always good for health. But I will continue this practice even after Id is over. I have little dal-bhat early in the morning and nothing else through out the day. Hunger and thirst are necessary for one's development."

He was sitting on a cushion and in front him on a small desk was an open tome. His body was arched over the desk and the sunlight slipped over his bare back.

" What are you reading?"

" This is Bible, the new revised standard version. It is used in churches all over India. Fathers refer to it."

Bhabhiji brought me a cushion and with all the warm clothing on me I struggled to sit on it.

" Just for a few minutes we will be here and then we can move to my study where you will be more comfortable."

" This is the King James version, this is the NIV Study Bible and this is another Reference", he said showing me other similar tomes.

" The same story may be told differently in different versions. One needs to study all of them. One needs to read between the lines to know the truth."

There were more Bibles in his study, even Hindi and Nepali versions. There were Korans, Vedas, Upanishads, Ramayana, Mahabharat, Guru Granth Sahib, collected works of Gandhi, Vivekananda, Aurobindo, Marx,Lenin.

" Nothing on Buddhism", I wondered aloud.

" There are books on Buddha. Must be somewhere else, I am not a very organised person, you know."

" But everything is contained in the Vedas. All other religions are just re-revelations. That does not mean that there is no need to study other religions. Only when you study all these you come to realise what I have just said. We are the lucky ones, the first people ever to get the revelations."

Bits of scribbled paper were pasted all over the walls. Some of them hung from the wooden frames of great men's photographs.

" These are the thoughts which suddenly come to me —————— observations, comments, quotations."

Then smiling: " when my maid comes to clean the room in the morning she often finds some of these lying on the floor. I tell her to keep them. They will be in great demand in future. She will become rich."

Like Uttam I too felt confused. Is he mad or is he a genius? I asked him why he is no longer a part of the political scenario.

" Politics has ceased to be my calling", he said with a finality.

" Uttam has joined SSP."

" Oh! Has he really?" There was a sense of desperation in his voice.

" Everybody says you are communal. That case you filed in the court ——— everybody still holds it against you."

" They have twisted it that way. I didn't ask for the reduction of BL seats. I asked for an increase in the total number of seats in the assembly so that the Sikkimese Nepalis would have more seats."

Reservation of seats for the Sikkimese Nepalis once again became a big issue in the election. They have been worst hit by the abolition of the Parity system. While earlier they had 15 reserved constituencies now they have to contest through 17 'general' seats. Way back in 1979 R.C in a letter to the Indian parliament had stated that due to the overwhelming influx of 'outsiders' into the state, " the Indian Sikkimese of Bhutia-Lepcha and Nepali origin will not be able to send our adequate representatives in the legislative assembly of Sikkim within a few years of time if our seats are not reserved." It remains a very contentious issue though no central government has as yet showed signs of addressing it. It will be no surprise if in the future an Assam-like, outsiders-hatao campaign explodes in Sikkim.

" You no longer make doomsday predictions?"

" Predictions cannot be made whenever one wishes. I know what you are hinting at", both of us burst out laughing.

" Actually one needs to work towards that kind of stature, attain that wisdom and that level of transcendence. It should be easier for us Indians, because as I told you, we were the first to receive the divine revelations."

Then he groped into his bookshelves and brought out a booklet.

" Even for writing one needs some religious knowledge. Read it whenever you like, no hurry."

It was 'My Master' by Swami Vivekananda, a compilation of two lectures he delivered in NewYork and England on Sri Ramakrishna Paramhansadev.

" We Hindus wasted our chance", he sighed.

" Look how other religions have progressed. It is difficult to get a decent translation of Vedas even in Hindi. But look at the zeal of the Christians. You can get translations of Bible even in tribal languages, and very good ones at that."

He has a point. Christmas is today an universal festival celebrated by people belonging to different religions and the expectancy with which my son looks for gifts under his pillow on Christmas day shows that the hugely popular Santa Claus is now also an Indian god.

" But India's time has come. It is now our time to rise", he said in a choked voice.

" Alkaganga will come down from the mountains and purify and purge the earth", he said rising from his seat, his hands skywards, as if he were a messiah just descended on earth.

" I have already had two visions, you know", he whispered standing, as if a zealot reading his sermons, a tantric weaving his spell.

There were moments of silence: A chilly breeze overturned pages of books, displaced his wrapper which hung limply on one of his shoulders.

" Don't take my last prediction too seriously. Yes, I was lacking then. I am waiting for the third vision after which I will attend *gyan bairagya*, enlightenment, sainthood, when everything worldly will cease to matter and I will dissolve among the people and lead them to the truth".

# Dusk at Khechodpalri

That third vision continues to elude R.C and he is still a recluse. Captain Yongda is still hardpressed to make some time for himself so that he could study the Treasure Texts which will enable him to perform miracles, cure even diseases like cancer and AIDS. Ironically two men who on that decisive day when the clash at Rangpo took place, stood facing each other, both fearless, resolute, unrelenting in their cause, have both today shifted far away from the humdrum of politics. Both have paid a heavy price for that momentous occasion which forever changed the face of Sikkim: while one has gone to jail several times for refusing to accept Sikkim as a part of India, the other after being in the centrestage of state politics for some years have been reviled and ridiculed as communal and a deshbechowa and pushed to isolation and sadhudom at his home in Asom Singtam. For both today politics has ceased to be the calling and Dharma is their only refuse.

Elsewhere Yabla talks of joining the mainstream. " We cannot live in the past, can we", he says. He is worried about the upkeep of his estate and is toying with the idea of starting a resort. Uttam is away in Delhi catching up with friends. That chamber of his which used to be our first stop on every visit to Gangtok is now locked. One day cricket tournaments are now held regularly at the Pelling ground. Nima still keeps lodgers at the bungalow waiting, screaming themselves hoarse, till he emerges phantom-like from the bushes. Gangtok has gone digital and cyber cafes and computer centres are mushrooming like anywhere else. The Sikkimese are eagerly looking forward to the day when the 17th Karmapa, Ogyen Trinley Dorjee, who had made a dramatic escape from Tibet and was staying at Dharamshala, would arrive in the state and take up his rightful place at the Rumtek monastery. Notwithstanding other claimants there is almost universal acceptance of the fourteen year boy as the new Karmapa. Trekkers full of tourists now go beyond Chhangoo, to Nathula from where they wave to Chinese soldiers. Suddenly leprosy is an issue and camps for its eradication are held. Faint, hesitant voices of feminism are surfacing in the local press. A langoor disrupts traffic in the capital. At Khechodpalri lake, clouds gather around the trees, darkness descends. Funnels of mosquitoes disperse, the zunkeri begins to sing, small ripples form in the placid lake. A Lepcha scantily dressed is scouring for forest produce. Dusk has set in but the lanky young man is still in search of his daily meal.